7 LESSONS FROM HEAVEN

7 LESSONS FROM HEAVEN

How Dying Taught Me to Live a Joy-Filled Life

MARY C. NEAL, M.D.

Author of *To Heaven and Back*

CONVERGENT

NEW YORK

Except where otherwise noted, I have used verses from the
New International Version of the Christian Bible.

In order to maintain the privacy of the people whose stories are included
in this book, I have taken the liberty of changing names and other
identifying details contained within them.

Copyright © 2017 by Mary C. Neal

All rights reserved.
Published in the United States by Convergent Books, an imprint of the
Crown Publishing Group, a division of Penguin Random House LLC,
New York.
crownpublishing.com

CONVERGENT BOOKS is a registered trademark and its C colophon is
a trademark of Penguin Random House LLC.

"Be Everything" by Regi Stone and Christy Sutherland copyright © 2009.
Experience Worship Music Publishing/ASCAP (admin. By ClearBox
Rights)/Mattmoosic (admin. by Capitol CMG Music Publishing/BMI).
All rights reserved. Used by permission.

Library of Congress Cataloging-in-Publication Data
Names: Neal, Mary C., author.
Title: 7 lessons from heaven / Mary C. Neal.
Other titles: Seven lessons from heaven
Description: New York : Convergent Books, 2017. | Includes
bibliographical references.
Identifiers: LCCN 2017009730 | ISBN 9780451495426 (tr)
Subjects: LCSH: Trust in God—Christianity. | Faith and reason—
Christianity. | Heaven—Christianity. | Thought and thinking—
Religious aspects—Christianity. | Religion and science. | Near-death
experiences—Religious aspects—Christianity.
Classification: LCC BV4637 .N43 2017 | DDC 231—dc23
LC record available at https://lccn.loc.gov/2017009730

ISBN 978-0-451-49542-6
Ebook ISBN 978-0-451-49543-3

Printed in the United States of America

Cover design by Alane Gianetti
Cover photograph by PHOTOCREO Michal Bednarek/Shutterstock

10 9 8 7 6 5 4 3 2 1

First Edition

*This book is dedicated to the God
who loves us more than we can fathom.*

Soli Deo Gloria

Contents

7 LESSONS FROM HEAVEN

Introduction

THIS CHANGES EVERYTHING

"To fall in love with God is the greatest of all romances;
to seek him, the greatest adventure;
to find him, the greatest human achievement."

—RAPHAEL SIMON

My story starts with me on the lip of a waterfall in South America, in that split second when you can see everything that is about to happen but know it's too late to change a thing. I was sitting in my kayak looking down and I knew I was in trouble. I knew I would be enveloped by the turbulence at the bottom, but also knew that I'd find a way out—I always had.

But this time was different. I didn't find my way out. After dropping into the roiling waters at the waterfall's base and plunging down six or eight feet below the water's surface, the nose of my boat became firmly wedged between some boulders at the bottom.

I immediately struggled to get free but no matter how hard I tried, nothing moved. The powerful torrents and weight of the water above kept me pinned facedown on the front deck of my kayak. My forceful efforts to escape this situation came to nothing and I knew that unless something changed or someone intervened, I would drown.

What happened next surprised even me. Time slowed and, despite knowledge of my predicament and the wild turbulence of the water above me, I felt relaxed, calm, and strangely hopeful. In that moment, I prayed words that seemed to come from outside myself. *God, your will be done. Not mine, but yours.*

I'll never know for sure, but in my heart I believe that's when my journey to heaven and back actually began.

You should know right from the start that I do not consider myself exceptional. I was then, as I am now, really quite ordinary. And yet, what happened as the water filled my lungs was truly extraordinary. I had a remarkable near-death experience (NDE) during which I saw the indescribable beauty of heaven, experienced Christ's overwhelming compassion, encountered angels, and was immersed in God's pure love.

Yes, that's saying a lot—and careful explanations will be forthcoming—but trust me, no one is more astonished by my words than I am.

As a surgeon, I had been conditioned by many years of medical training to be skeptical of anything beyond the scientific realm. If it couldn't be measured, probed, x-rayed, and reproduced, then I couldn't rationally accept it. That's why, in the months following my drowning and the supernatural experiences that followed, I fervently searched for a nonspiritual explanation for it all.

But there was none. After much research, I came to the undeniable conclusion that most of my experience fell utterly outside the boundaries of medicine and science.

Still, I hesitated. Call it pride, professional skepticism, or running away from what I knew God was asking me to do. Whatever you call it, it took me many years to break through my own resistance and begin talking about my experiences in public. But the truth is, I had been given an assignment in heaven, and I was expected to share my story with others. Usually I refer to that assignment as a mandate—a heavenly commission of great importance. When I finally rose to the task, I wrote *To Heaven and Back,* which described as best as I could at the time what had happened.

As you might expect, describing heavenly and spiritual experiences is difficult. I have heard other people with NDEs echo what I have often said: There are simply no earthly words to describe heavenly wonders. Even the most transcendent words in our language fall short. That's because the sensations of heaven are greater in number and intensity, and the sense of time and dimension is so radically different from what we experience or understand here on Earth.

As a result, many of my descriptions in *To Heaven and Back* struck me later as inadequate and incomplete. I am embarrassed to admit that I mostly wrote that book to remove it from my "to do" list so I could move on to other things.

But I learned, as I often do, that God's plans are much bigger than my own. I have now had the opportunity to share my story throughout the world, and I've had the great privilege of speaking to thousands of people about life, death, spiritual experiences, and miracles. In turn, I have heard hundreds of stories of NDEs, dream visitations, divine intervention, and miracles. I have shared tears with countless people who are grieving the loss of loved ones. And as I've told my story, I have realized again and again that there is so much more to tell that can be of help to other people.

Wherever I go, I hear the same questions: *Can you describe more details of what you saw? I'm still reeling over the loss of a loved one—what can you tell me that might bring me some hope and consolation? What did you hear or learn while you were in heaven? Are angels real? How is your life different today?*

I know now is the time to answer those questions—to fulfill not just the requirements of my heavenly assignment, but to bring as much science, faith, and life experience to the telling as possible. And most importantly of all, to tell why it matters for someone else. You, for example. That's why I am writing this book.

If you haven't read my story in *To Heaven and Back,* don't worry—in the coming pages I'll catch you up on what happened. I won't recap every detail, but I will share enough that you won't feel lost in the story. If you *have* read my story in *To Heaven and Back,* you will quickly see that this book is different.

My first book primarily focused on what happened. I started with my childhood, tracing my journey to faith through my years in higher education and my life as a practicing orthopedic surgeon in Jackson Hole, Wyoming. I told about the kayaking trip to Chile, my drowning, my near-death experience, and my recovery. And I told about the death of my son Willie and what it was like to experience that loss in the aftermath of my accident.

This book primarily focuses on "so what?" What difference has my NDE made in my life? And more importantly, what difference could it make in yours? How can my experiences help you navigate your life more joyfully?

Part One begins with a quick retelling of my story—because if you haven't read *To Heaven and Back,* I don't want you to feel left out. But I share missing pieces of my story about my journey to heaven, including details of what I saw and felt, and most importantly, a careful retelling of two conversations with Jesus. In both, I experienced his unconditional love, compassion, and kindness. I also learned about heavenly time and forgiveness.

Woven into these chapters are seven life-altering insights,

or lessons, that I brought back from heaven. I will show you that not only does life go beyond science, but that as spiritual beings, we inhabit an angel-filled world in which miracles abound. In exploring God's plan for us and how to discern it, I will discuss how beauty can arise from all things and I will show you that we can live with joy, even in the midst of loss.

In Part Two, I present a practical and life-tested way to live differently with the beautiful truths of heaven in mind. I call this living with absolute trust. By that I mean, you and I aren't supposed to simply press on in the *hope* that God's promises are true, or even a general belief in or *faith* that God's promises are true. Instead, we're invited to thrive in *absolute trust* that God is good, His promises are true, and we can trust Him completely with our lives now and forever.

Moving from hope to absolute trust will radically change what you feel, think, and believe. Most of all, it leads us to what most of us have always wanted anyway—a joy-filled life. We just try to get there by following paths that lead nowhere. In the final chapter, I show you how to keep your focus on trust and why living with absolute trust holds so much promise for joy in your life.

The wonderful news is that living in absolute trust is not just for people who have visited heaven. It's meant for everyone, and I believe God means it to change how we live in very practical ways: how we welcome success, face challenges, process the death of a loved one, approach our daily work, raise our children, interact with people around us, and pursue our dreams. And I will show you how to make this transformation.

Are there obstacles to face on this journey? Of course, and I will talk about those candidly. Yet as we explore all this in the pages ahead, my deepest desire is that you will come away knowing what I now know—that at all times, we live inside

God's embrace. I know that now. We are never alone. We are never less than entirely and forever loved.

As you read these words, I invite you to open your heart to the possibility that God wants to use my story to shine His great love into even the most shadowed places in your soul, showing you how to embrace a life of greater peace, meaning, and joy than you have ever known.

If my journey from the bottom of a river to the heights of heaven revealed anything to me, it is that God is not only real and present in our world, but that He knows each one of us by name, loves each one of us as though we were the only person on Earth, and has a plan for each of us that is more significant and rewarding than anything we can dare to imagine on our own.

I hope you turn the page.

PART ONE

Chapter 1

RIVER OF DEATH,
RIVER OF LIFE

"Death is not the end of life;
it is the beginning of an eternal journey."

—Debasish Mridha

Good friends, sunshine, and the beautiful outdoors—that January morning in 1999 began with the same excitement and anticipation I had felt on countless previous kayaking adventures I had shared with my husband, Bill. It was our final day before returning to the United States, and it was my husband's birthday. We planned to celebrate by paddling in a remote part of Chile, on an infrequently run portion of the upper Fuy River known for its many waterfalls. As experienced whitewater kayakers, Bill and I knew the ten- to fifteen-foot falls would be challenging, but well within our skill set.

We'd be paddling with Tom, a professional raft and kayak guide who had been leading trips in Chile for more than twenty years, his two adult sons, Chad and Kenneth, and Kenneth's wife, Anne, as well as several other clients.

This stretch of the Fuy requires focus and a complete commitment. That's because, in addition to being in a remote part of Chile, the river is often closed in on both banks by steep hillsides made impassable by dense bamboo forests. This topography makes getting off the river sooner than the designated downstream take-out point extremely challenging, if not impossible. Once you start down the river, there's no turning back.

When Bill uncharacteristically awoke that morning with severe back pain, he made the difficult and disappointing decision not to kayak with us that day. Instead, he dropped us off at the river, giving me his bright red paddling jacket to wear beneath my equally bright red life jacket, kissed me good-bye, and told me to be safe. He planned to find a sunny spot to spend the day reading, intending to meet us downstream at the end of the day. It felt strange going without Bill, but I couldn't wait to get started.

As our group pushed off, I moved out of the eddy, confidently paddling my kayak forward into the swiftly moving river. We didn't know that disaster would strike within minutes.

Ahead of us were two waterfalls. I moved toward the smaller one, which our group had agreed would provide the safest descent into the waters below. But as I approached this waterfall, I could see that someone else's kayak was lodged sideways in its entrance, and the powerful current was pulling me straight toward them. I had to act quickly.

With no other option, I veered away, only to be propelled straight toward the larger waterfall. I would have to make the best of it. As I was thrust over the lip of the waterfall, I saw tremendous turbulence below. In a flash, I pictured what would come.

At the bottom, I would flip upside down. The turbulence would keep me from being able to right myself, so I would have to detach the neoprene spray skirt that was keeping me dry before I could push myself out of my boat. I'd get tumbled around by the chaotic waters and claw my way to the surface while being flushed downstream. Then, gasping for air, I'd swim to shore and sheepishly begin collecting my belongings. What can I say—most whitewater kayakers have endured it at least once. I prepared myself for the inevitable.

But what I assumed would happen did not.

I rapidly dropped into the turbulence below and, predictably, plunged deep below the water's surface. But then I came to a sudden and sickening stop when the front end of my boat became jammed in the underwater features. I remained upright in my boat instead of being flipped upside down, but instead of quickly popping back to the surface, I was stuck under six to eight feet of water that quickly closed over my head.

I tried vainly to rock my kayak free. Then I tried to free myself from the boat. But the sheer weight of the water overhead and the force of the current bent my torso forward and kept even my arms pinned to the front deck of my kayak. I had no air pocket and no time to spare. No matter how hard I tried, my efforts to move were laughable. And I began to realize then what would actually happen.

I would drown.

SLIPPING AWAY

I had always imagined that drowning would be a terrible and terrifying way to die, and I took note that instead of experiencing terror, I actually felt quite peaceful. I experienced no air hunger, no panic, and no fear. And I began to calmly pray. Oddly, I didn't beg God to rescue me. Instead, I prayed only, "Your will be done."

It wasn't about giving up. It was more about actively turning toward God. That's why I often say, God did not *take* my future—I willingly *gave* it to Him.

The moment I relinquished my future to God's will, I felt the physical sensation of being held and comforted by Jesus. I don't mean this in an abstract, greeting-card kind of way. I felt his embrace as tangibly as I could feel the plastic of the boat around my legs and the weight of the water pressing on my torso.

As I wrote in *To Heaven and Back,* Jesus assured me that everything was "fine," that my husband would be "fine," and my young children would be "fine," regardless of whether I lived or died. It felt as though Jesus was pouring his boundless love, kindness, compassion, and mercy into my very soul.

Time seemed to stop. I sensed my spirit expanding and becoming a part of everything around me. I felt connected to everything. Time for me could have ended at that moment and I would have been more than content. But Jesus was with me. It was during this time that Jesus lovingly showed me the story of my life and reminded me of the great beauty that comes of all events. (In the pages ahead, I'll talk more about life reviews.)

While I was basking in the bottomless kindness and compassion of Jesus, my kayaking friends had figured out that I was under the water below the falls. They became increasingly desperate in their attempts to reach me, but nothing was working.

The dying process seemed to be taking a very long time and, although I had no sense of my friends' efforts, I could feel the powerful currents pulling my body out and over the front deck of my boat. Eventually, the current ripped my helmet from my head and my life jacket from my body. My knees were forced to bend forward, breaking bones and tearing ligaments in the process, yet I felt no pain.

As my body was leaving my boat, I could also feel something else happening—Jesus was releasing me, and my spirit was slowly separating from my body. Suddenly, I felt my spirit release with a small pop. The separation felt painless, gentle, and beautiful. I never experienced being conscious one moment and unconscious the next. Instead, I felt conscious and then *more* conscious. I had a heightened clarity and intensity of consciousness, and I felt more alive than I had ever felt.

My body finally broke free from my kayak and was dragged downstream, sometimes bumping and scraping along the bottom of the river, sometimes tumbling in the current. But I don't remember any of that. What I do remember is this: gracefully rising up out of the river, feeling freedom and lightness as the water fell away from my outstretched arms, and feeling the brilliant sunshine that seemed to pull me upward . . . until I could look down on the entire scene.

I was not afraid. With God's perfect love so profoundly present, fear had no room to exist.

As I hovered above the river, I was welcomed by a group of "somethings." Perhaps I should call them people, spirits, angels, or soul friends. But these words mean different things to different people, so I am never quite sure what to call the beings who welcomed me. All I can say is that I had absolute knowledge that these beings had known me and loved me as long as I had existed, and that I had known and loved them also. I believe if I had looked closely at those in my welcoming committee, I would have recognized each of them as someone who had been important in my life experience, regardless of whether I had known them on Earth or not. For example, one might have been a great-grandparent who died long before I was born.

But here's the important thing. They were radiant, brilliant, and overflowing with God's love. In that moment, I knew without a doubt that they had been sent by God to comfort, guide, and protect me. In their presence, I felt completely and unconditionally loved by God in a way that is elusive if not impossible on Earth. I was filled with an inexpressible peace and joy that made life on Earth seem pale and unappealing by comparison.

I felt like I had finally returned home.

TURNING TOWARD HEAVEN

But I still hadn't left Earth. Not yet. I found myself reveling in my new existence but still watching what was happening on the river below. Yes, a different sense of time and dimension existed in this world I had entered. The past, present, and future all seemed to merge into one reality. I seemed to be in a different spacial dimension as well. But all the while, I was able to look down on the scene at the river.

By now, I had been under the water for almost thirty minutes.

Downstream, my bright red life jacket bobbed to the surface, catching the attention of Tom's eighteen-year-old son, Chad, who quickly jumped into the river to retrieve it. As he swam toward shore, he felt something bump into his leg. It was my body. Serenely, I watched as he grabbed my wrist and pulled my lifeless body from the water.

Later, observing my friends begin CPR, I came to the full realization that I must be dead. Surprisingly, this did not provoke concern or sadness in me—I simply took note of it. On the riverbank, one of the other kayakers encouraged my friends to stop CPR. Too much time had passed since I had drowned, she said. She warned that if they were able to revive me, I would "just be a vegetable." Another kayaker wanted to videotape everything. Another panicked and ran up the hillside and out of sight.

My friends below were frantically focused, but I felt calm.

I thought about what a delightful and wonderfully rich life I had lived in my body. It had been a life of opportunity, adventure, and growth. I had a loving husband and four precious young children who expanded my heart beyond what I would have imagined possible, dear family and friends, and a fulfilling job. I had loved deeply and been loved deeply in return. But as I watched the events play out on the riverbank, I felt certain that I was now home and that my life in that body was over.

And honestly, I did not want to return. Today, I am a little chagrined to admit my lack of desire to return, knowing the grief my family would have endured. But if you think about what I was experiencing in those moments, perhaps you will understand. I was getting my first taste of our true home in God's love.

Swept up in that love, I gratefully acknowledged the life that had been mine, then silently said good-bye and turned away from the riverbank in the direction of heaven.

I began to move with my guides up a path to the entrance of a great domed structure that I knew was the point of no return. As we gently traveled, my companions and I communicated without words and moved without walking. We didn't speak using our mouths to form words, but the communication was pure and clear. I heard the communication in English, my native language, but it was as if the words were being sent from one person to another in their most elemental form, just transference of energy and meaning.

Our travel was not instantaneous, but we moved gracefully and effortlessly. I don't know if I actually had feet, and never even thought to look. The path we traveled seemed like a physical surface—it looked like a solid surface—but it existed in the midst of nothing. The indistinct edges of the road, as well as the space above and below the road, expanded into the universe. With no beginning or end, this path was inexplicably beautiful.

The colors of nature and the magnificent aromas of flowers and trees have always touched me deeply and, not surprisingly, this is what I began to encounter. As I looked more closely, the path we were on seemed to be stitched together with every color of the rainbow and even some colors I'd never seen before. A seemingly infinite variety of flowers sprouted along the edges of the path, and my very being was infused with their sumptuous aroma. The array and vividness of the colors, the intricacies of the flowers, and the allure of the aromas were all far more intense than anything I have seen or experienced on Earth. I not only saw and smelled these things, but also heard, tasted, and felt them. My senses expanded, and I could both experience them and understand them.

Of course, I realize this description is difficult to fathom, but I felt that I was a part of the beauty, and it was a part of me. And overlaying and saturating all of this was God's palpable, complete, unwavering, and all-encompassing love. It was a greater love than I had ever understood or experienced. Even now the feeling is impossible to put into words. I never wanted to leave.

AT THE THRESHOLD

I may not have wanted to leave, but far below me on the riverbank, Tom, Kenneth, and Chad were doing everything in their power to thwart my intentions. While Tom and his sons performed CPR, I could hear Chad pleading with me to come back and "take a breath." Hearing his urgency, I glanced backward and was struck by the vulnerable expression on this young man's face. Overcome with compassion, I traveled back down the path to my body, where I lay down in my body and took a single breath before getting up to rejoin my companions and travel farther up the path.

But then I heard Chad pleading again. "Come on! I know you are still here. Breathe! Just one more breath!" Again, I felt compelled to return to my body and take one more breath. My return to take a single breath, which is how I quite literally interpreted his pleading, occurred repeatedly as we slowly made our way up the path. Again and again and again our progress along the path was delayed as I retuned for another breath in response to Chad's calling.

The souls accompanying me never scolded me, hurried me, or expressed anything but pure love and understanding at these interruptions. As the journey continued, we finally reached the arched threshold of the great domelike structure.

This structure was so large that I could not see its edges and, like the path we were walking on, it had no distinct edges. It appeared to be solid, although I never actually touched it or leaned against it.

Standing beneath the arched opening, I looked around. The archway was tall, but not very wide, and it might have been about ten feet deep. I was able to stand there with one of the people in my group, while the others crowded around us. The archway seemed to be constructed of large blocks woven together with fibers of God's love. Like everything else, the structure was brilliant but not blinding, nor did its radiance cast shadows. I wonder if these could have been the clichéd "pearly gates"? Although the bricks did not look to be literally made of pearl, I could imagine that someone might use that analogy to describe the lustrous play of iridescent light emanating from within each block, from the core of their existence.

I looked beyond the arch and into the center of the dome,

where I could see a great deal of activity and many, many beings bustling about. They were too many to count and were
moving along different pathways, going in and out of other
structures. Was I seeing the heavenly Jerusalem mentioned in
scripture? Maybe. These other buildings were tall and just as
ethereal as the domed structure. They too seemed to radiate
love from within their core.

I had the impression that most of the beings were people,
although some seemed to be angels. I'm not sure why I had
this impression and can't specifically identify what the difference really was, but the ones I thought were angels seemed
larger and more glorious, if that were possible. I have no
idea what everyone was busy doing. Perhaps I was seeing
the "thousands upon thousands of angels in joyful assembly"
of Hebrews 12:22, because I remember that their pure joy
seemed to create a beautiful melodic hum. Like those who
had greeted and guided me, these "people" struck me as ageless, healthy, vibrant, and strong. As I stood watching I was
filled with awe and wonder.

Hours passed, or so it seemed to me, and during that time,
I experienced a profound sense of universal understanding.
Finally, everything just made sense. All I had to do was think
of a question or subject, no matter how complex, and I immediately understood the answer. I not only understood the
answer, but I understood the basis for the answer. I was able
to observe the complexity of the universe, and yet I understood its truth.

While I no longer remember most of the questions I asked,
nor their answers, and did not return with a new understanding of quantum physics, I am left with the memory of how I
was able to see that everything is logical, interconnected, and
divinely ordered. Indeed, we are all connected, forming one

body. Above all, I retained a deep understanding of the truth of many of God's promises, all of which lead us to joy.

But something turned me back toward Earth.

TO STAY OR TO GO

Ultimately, it was not Chad's pleadings or anyone else's efforts that brought me back. It was, I believe, the will of God. Despite my joy at being "home," the souls accompanying me told me that it was not my time. They said I had more work to do on Earth, and that I would need to return to my body. I assured them, as Jesus had assured me, that everything would be fine if I stayed, but they were adamant. To convince me, they gently began to tell me about some of the work I still needed to do on Earth.

One of the more heartbreaking things they shared had to do with the future death of my oldest son. I was told that Willie, then just nine years old, would die "soon," and that I was to use my own near-death experience to help others see the beauty of his life and of his death.

This did not surprise me, as my son had told me many years earlier that he would die young, and I now believe his telling me was a gift of preparation so I could listen and not panic when the souls shared these things with me in heaven.

"But why?" I asked with a broken heart. "Why *my* son? And why so soon?"

I was immediately taken back to the life review and reminded of what Jesus promised me—that I could always count on God's love, and trust that His plan for each person, and for the world, is one of hope.

That's when I was led back down the path, toward my lifeless body lying on the wet, rocky banks of the river.

Chapter 2

SEEING MY LIFE FROM OUTSIDE TIME

"Hours were made for man, not man for hours."

—FRANÇOIS RABELAIS

Ever since I was born, I had experienced time as flowing in linear fashion from the past, to the present, to the future. Like most people in the Western world, I'm a linear, schedule-driven person who relies on clocks to organize my busy life. Thinking about time in this way always provided me a sense of control and a way to map out a path to the future I desired.

Time has been a commodity to be used, spent, budgeted, and saved. Sometimes I have felt like I have a timer in my head. Not literally, of course, but seconds continually tick off, just as they do after the start of a race. Sometimes that is helpful, like when I am beginning a precisely planned surgical procedure where efficiency is important and timing is crucial, but sometimes it can interfere with the experience of the moment.

One . . . Two . . . Three . . . It's an almost physical sensation.

If you are like I am, then I'm guessing that you've already been internally timing my story, subconsciously testing it at every turn.

So how many minutes was she in the kayak before she drowned?

When she had that conversation with the heavenly beings, how much time did that take?

And, let's see, does this really add up?

But heaven doesn't work that way. My journey to heaven and back turned my understanding of time inside out. Time as I had always known it really did end the moment I passed from my earthly life to the afterlife. What had been counted out in seconds, minutes, hours, or years—all in a straight line from the past into the future—became something else.

It felt more like a vast web, where time and space were connected. Counting time didn't make sense anymore. Everything past, present, and future seemed to be happening in the here and now. Let me try to explain.

PART OF ETERNITY

While trapped underwater, I was still quite conscious of linear time, perceiving its passage and recognizing that I would likely die as a result. But I also simultaneously felt like I was a part of the past and the future. I felt a part of eternity.

Eternity is a very long time, and some people anxiously worry that heaven will be terribly boring. After a few centuries of exploring heaven's wonders, won't we start to get bored? Popular imagery—often so egregiously misguided—depicts heaven as an endless church service, where we will listen to organ music and sing dirgelike hymns forevermore. Or, worse yet, we'll sit on clouds all day playing harps. Some might think this is a perfect way to spend time without end, but not many. No wonder so many people are uncomfortable thinking about eternity.

What I discovered is that heavenly time—the thing we call eternity—is more like a place in which you dwell rather than a line down which you walk. It blossoms rather than passes. It's something to be experienced rather than spent. (Are you still with me?)

So, for example, eternity isn't really an infinite number of years lined up in a row where one year turns into the next, and one century into another—like chapters in a history book. All of time—past, present, and future—is *right here, right now.*

For me, every moment contained its past, present, and future as it expanded into all of eternity, and I experienced all of eternity in each single moment. I instantaneously felt a part of nothing and of everything.

I discovered that time is enjoyed completely in *this moment.* So there are no thoughts in heaven about what might happen tomorrow or next year or next century. The present moment is as rich and satisfying as we can possibly imagine.

Time ended for me when I was under the water. You could say I realized experientially what Albert Einstein realized intellectually—that time is relative and should be considered a fourth dimension. One biblical writer put it this way: "With the Lord, a day is like a thousand years, and a thousand years are like a day" (2 Peter 3:8).

If your internal clock is working, you've already experienced some anxiety about time passing as I've told you my story. Down on the riverbank the seconds never stopped ticking away, while at the same time my experience in heaven seemed to unfold in complete serenity and with little bearing on what was happening around my body.

For me, the differences in how we experience time were never more clear than during my so-called "life review," which occurred while I was underwater, slipping across the threshold between life and death.

REWIND AND REVIEW

Everyone is familiar with Judgment Day. Most of us assume it will be a time when good deeds are rewarded and bad deeds are punished. This image fills most of us with dread at one time or another. We imagine God sitting on an enormous jewel-encrusted golden throne meting out judgment to an endless line of cowering humans, each waiting his or her turn. This is the fear and frustration reflected in humanist Walt Whitman's statement that "God is a mean-spirited, pugnacious bully bent on revenge against his children for failing to live up to his impossible standards."

Like most people, before experiencing my own, I would have imagined a life review to merely be a prelude to this final judgment by God. Despite my goals and efforts to lead a moral, ethical, and "good" life, I would have anticipated that my own life review would be filled primarily with regret, disappointment, and guilt. Despite grasping for the hope presented in the life review of George Bailey in the movie *It's a Wonderful Life,* most of us feel undeserving of grace, Christians included.

But I learned that a "life review" isn't that sort of experience at all, and most people who have been through an NDE report the same thing. In fact, it is often the most enlightening event a person ever experiences. Typically, a "being of light," who is often identified as Christ, God, "Source," or "pure love," presents the dying person with a review of their entire life. Regardless of whether this review is perceived as a panorama, a movie, or in small segments, it is always infused with understanding and compassion. And quite often, invaluable learning.

For example, some people are given the opportunity to "relive" experiences from a variety of perspectives. This often teaches the dying person about himself or others, yields an understanding of why he, she, or others are the way they are, and exposes the motives of everyone involved. Just as it did for the movie character George Bailey, reliving experiences also reveals the impact of the dying person's words and actions on others, and it often leads them to a greater sense of purpose. People usually come away from a life review with a powerful sense of how they are indelibly intertwined with the universe and connected to all other people and living creatures, and they hold fast to the unshakable belief that love is the most important aspect of life.

I've noticed it doesn't matter how young the believer is, or how long and earnestly he or she has strived to follow God. We all suffer from comparison to some ideal. When we look at others, we realize that we don't pray enough, we don't volunteer enough, we don't give enough, we don't love enough, and the list goes on. We feel that no matter how hard we try, our contributions on this earth pale in comparison with so many others who have done so much more. I get it. We forget that we each make little and large important contributions to the whole every day. We forget, too, what we might have experienced in moments of deepest surrender to God. In any case, it's only human to worry that when our life is laid bare before God, our faults, weaknesses, and darkest secrets will render us unworthy of his forgiveness and reward.

But let me tell you what happened to me.

I was gently leaning into Jesus, embraced and comforted by his presence. Scenes from my life became visible in front of us, as though projected onto a large three-dimensional multisensory screen. Everything else that may have surrounded us faded into irrelevancy. Rather than anxiety or apprehension, I felt nothing but love. When I looked into Jesus's face, I saw only kindness in endless supply. In His arms, I felt like a newborn baby into whom He poured all of His hope, concern, love, and His very being. His embrace was gentle, complete, and familiar. As my life unspooled before me, I felt deeply loved, and I knew somehow that His love was not just for me, but for all people.

The scenes moved quickly past, from right to left in sequential order. It was like swiping through the chain at the bottom of "all photos" on an iPhone. This forward motion intermittently slowed when Jesus reached his hand forward to pluck a scene from the strand of my life. Rather than just seeing the scene in front of me, I would immediately reexperience it with absolute understanding, and from every vantage point.

If this sounds impossible to you, remember the paradigm shift I laid out at the top of this chapter: Time seemed to no longer exist. I was alive in the eternal present. And everything existed in and because of the love of God. In other words, I tasted the eternity of goodness and grace that awaits us all.

As I looked at each aspect of a scene or event, I was able to instantaneously see the life story of the people involved. I perfectly understood their emotional backgrounds, motivations, and feelings. I understood their side of the story, what they brought to the situation, and how we were each changed by it.

Things got specific. The rage and confusion I felt as a child when I was witness to physical violence was replaced by compassion as I saw how the hurts, expectations, and hopes of the people involved had brought them to that moment. Their personal history influenced their behavior and reactions, and I saw how that moment would transform the future. The decades-old anger I felt toward a neighbor boy who had physically molested me as a young girl dissolved into empathy and forgiveness. Again and again, seeing a person's backstory—their experiences, circumstances, sorrows—changed my understanding of them and my emotional response became one of grace.

My life review actually reset my understanding of grace, and I think it can do the same for you.

Grace is often thought of somewhat dismissively as just an empty and unattainable cliché. As we listen to the lies of our broken past, we assume that grace is reserved only for others. But God's New Testament grace is relational and is the manifestation of His promised love for *each* of us. He looks beyond our flaws and failing, accepting us just as we are. Where we see only brokenness, He sees restoration and healing.

God's grace is His love in action—continual forgiveness, encouragement, mercy, compassion, and kindness that is borne out of undeserved love.

That is what I learned about the grace that God offers. And it doesn't end with us. The grace we accept is also the grace that we are able to offer others, regardless of what the circumstances might be.

THE FIRST LESSON THAT HEAVEN REVEALS

Circumstances make sense when seen through heaven's lens, and the abundant grace we receive from God is the same grace we can freely offer others.

As you can imagine, an experience like that changes you. I'm not the same person I used to be. I experience much more grace toward others, even in minor situations. When I feel cheated or taken advantage of, even when an erratic driver cuts me off in traffic, I am able to feel a gentleness toward the perpetrator that I didn't before. When someone treats me rudely or disrespectfully, I remind myself that the person is, at that moment, the sum total of all his or her burdens and joys, successes, and failures. Certainly, I feel all the strong emotions that come with being human, but now I'm better able to choose how to respond.

It shows up in large and small ways.

Once, I suddenly left the wedding of a friend's son as his parents were walking down the aisle. Several days later I overheard someone make an unkind remark about how rude my behavior had been. Here's the context: I had thought it important to attend the wedding because the groom had been a classmate and friend of my son Willie. It was a happy occasion, and everyone was beaming. But it was the first wedding I had attended since my son's death, and when I saw the groom's smiling parents, I was unexpectedly overcome with a deep sense of loss at never being able to share this sort of event with Willie. I left quickly to avoid distracting others with my tears.

But others couldn't know that, right? In that instance at least, I was able to look at the unkind response differently. With the big picture in mind. With kindness instead of a grudge.

RIPPLE EFFECTS

As Jesus "swiped" through the scenes of my life, I witnessed how certain actions rippled outward from the original incident, like concentric circles, to affect others. It is easy to understand how our words and actions impact our immediate circle of family and friends, but it is usually impossible to appreciate their distant influence. During the review of my life, Jesus repeatedly allowed me to see both the immediate and distant effects of an event. I was able to appreciate and understand how each event spread through time and space, initiating a cascade of other events from which something of beauty and worth always emerged.

I did *not* feel grateful or happy when my parents realized their marriage was unworkable and divorced. The foundation of my world crumbled. I was left feeling wounded, betrayed, abandoned, angry, and ashamed. And when my prayers for their reconciliation went unanswered, I felt abandoned by God, too, and discarded my childhood notions of a loving heavenly Father. At the time, and for many years after, nothing would have convinced me that something good would, or even could, come of such a rotten situation.

Yet one of God's most astonishing gifts is His ability to use time to heal and redeem: to make something beautiful later out of something that appears ugly now. In my case, the man who eventually became my stepfather became one of my life's greatest and most cherished influences. Through his example and guidance, he taught me about humility, unconditional love, patience, steadfastness, and compassion. Now, despite the pain I felt at the time, I see the dissolution of my parents' marriage differently. If the breakup hadn't happened, George would never have come into my life.

Does God really work all things together for our good? During my life review, as I witnessed beauty emerging from every event, my faith in God's promise shifted from a somewhat vague theological hope into complete trust. I understood that He genuinely does make everything beautiful in His time.

I don't say this lightly, and I will explore it more later. You or those you know and love could be facing unimaginably difficult and painful obstacles today. No matter how charmed life can seem, that day will come for most of us. I hope the experiences in my life review will bring encouragement and confidence to you.

Events that seem horrible and unjust do indeed ripple outward and touch people in positive ways—in ways that we would never imagine from our earthly perspective, but will be perfectly evident when we see them from heaven.

The secret, in the meanwhile, is to allow ourselves to be transformed by trust. As I'll show you in a later chapter, consciously choosing to trust God's promises opens the door to fully experiencing the depth of God's love, grace, and His very presence in the world. Even in times of struggle and heartache, we can expectantly wait for the beauty that will surely come.

The change in my perspective, and the powerful feeling of being so deeply loved by God, was still fresh before my eyes as I began to feel the force of the flowing water pulling my body over the front deck of my boat. As I felt Jesus slowly release me, he told me to remember what I had been shown.

My life review had come to a close, but its impact would ripple through my life in countless ways.

Chapter 3

WE ARE BOTH PHYSICAL AND SPIRITUAL BEINGS

"The boundaries which divide Life from Death are at best
shadowy and vague.
Who shall say where the one ends and the other begins?"

—Edgar Allan Poe

Every description of a near-death experience includes a moment when there is a separation of spirit from body. You might have heard folks say this can't happen, that body and spirit can't be separated, that when your body is dead, it's done. Turn out the lights, the party's over.

And yet my own experience resoundingly tells me otherwise.

I used to think of myself as a physical being capable of spiritual experiences, like feeling loved or feeling moved by "soulful" experiences. What I discovered when I stopped being a "physical being" was that my capacity for experiencing everything around me—including and especially the profound love of God for me—radically expanded.

Actually, I have never felt more alive than when I left my body far behind.

There is no doubt that we are both physical and spiritual beings. When we look more deeply at spiritual events com-

monly surrounding a person's death, we realize there's a rich
and reliable treasury of stories of other kinds of out-of-body
experiences—deathbed visions and visitations, for example,
and a sudden awareness that as much as we identify with our
bodies, we are *more* than our bodies. That's what this chapter
is about.

Don't you think it's a wonderful paradox, and a gift from
a loving God, that just as people arrive at the threshold between life and death, heaven seems to break through all
around? Old ways of organizing reality come up short. God
seems more tangibly present, and more insistent on showing
us that his loving plans for us are so much grander than what
we had supposed.

The following poem captures the richness and mystery
that greets souls in that moment of departure and arrival.
"What is dying?" he wrote. "I am standing on the seashore.
A ship sails to the morning breeze and starts for the ocean.
She is an object and I stand watching her until she fades from
the horizon and someone at my side says, 'She is gone!' Gone
where? Gone from my sight, that is all. Her diminished size
and loss of sight is in me, not in her. And just at the moment
when someone at my side says, 'She is gone!' there are others
who are watching her coming, gladly shouting, 'Here she
comes!'—and that is dying."

AS THE SOUL IS DEPARTING

When I left my body underwater, I felt like my spirit was
slowly peeling itself away, sort of like taking off a heavy wet
shirt. The river current was pulling my physical self downstream, and the brilliance of the sun was pulling my spiritual self upward. From my spiritual self, I could see my body
going over the front deck of my boat. I didn't try to stop this

separation and don't think I could have anyway. I still felt like myself and was acutely aware of my circumstances.

In fact, I repeatedly did mental self-assessment exams to see how I was feeling. When I both felt and saw my knees bending back upon themselves, I took a moment to ponder the question of consciousness. Was I screaming, or feeling pain? No. Was I trying to breathe or swim? No. At least it didn't feel like it. What I did feel was my spiritual self being lifted out of the river. As I was pulled higher and higher, I felt light and free.

I often joke that I am a lizard at heart—I come alive and feel a deep sense of happiness and contentment when I feel bright sunshine warming my skin. This is exactly how I felt as my spiritual self left my boat. The warmth of the bright light, which I perceived as a beautiful orb set in a deep blue sky, seemed to envelop me and give me life. In fact, I had the impression that this sun was the source of all life and of all love. It was beckoning to me, and I willingly rose to meet it.

The distinction between body and soul is noted as far back as the book of Genesis. As Jacob was traveling with his family and servants, Jacob's beloved wife, Rachel, went into a very difficult labor. The son who was born survived, but Rachel died in childbirth. We read, "And as her soul was departing (for she was dying), she called his name Ben-oni" (Genesis 35:18; English Standard Version).

As her soul was departing. That description resonates deeply with me, for that is exactly what I experienced. The "pop" or "plop" I felt when my spiritual self finally shook free of my physical body was like the sound water makes after a stone drops in.

In Ecclesiastes, we find another description of the spirit as a very separate entity from the body. But this reference compares the mysteries of the spirit arriving in the body with the mysteries of understanding how God works. Solomon declares, "As you do not know how the spirit comes to the bones in the womb of a woman with child, so you do not know the work of God who makes everything" (11:5; Revised Standard Edition).

What a fascinating picture of the distinctiveness of body and spirit! Yes, there is a moment they come together but before that moment, they are separate, and how it all happens we simply don't know.

In the next chapter in Ecclesiastes 12:7, the writer describes the process of death in terms of spirit departing the body: "And the dust returns to the ground it came from, and the spirit returns to God who gave it." Later in the Bible, Paul explains that we leave our earthly bodies behind when we go to heaven, exchanging them for eternal bodies made for us by God (1 Corinthians 15). And in 2 Corinthians 5, he describes the body as a "tent," and notes that when we are at home in our body, we are away from the Lord, but when we are away from the body, we are at home with the Lord.

In all this arriving and departing, did you notice what endures? Only the spirit is eternal. "We are not human beings having a spiritual experience," wrote the French philosopher and Jesuit priest Pierre Teilhard de Chardin. "We are spiritual beings having a human experience."[1] Nothing in his writings suggests he had an NDE, yet I wholeheartedly agree with his written sentiment.

My own experience tells me that we are mostly spirit encased in an "earth suit." Yes, as a surgeon, I marvel at the wonders of the human body as God created it. But I am even more amazed at the spirit residing within that body. Our spirits—much more than the tissues, nerves, and bones that make up our bodies—are the very essence of who we are.

Maybe that's why so many people—from the very religious

to the not religious at all—see and hear the miraculous when they are close to the very moment of leaving this earth.

DEATHBED VISIONS

Health-care providers and family members are also frequent witnesses to what are called "deathbed visions," in which the dying person often seems to be preparing for his or her departure and may look or reach toward something, unseen by others, before their physical death. Perhaps they are seeing or grasping the hand of someone who has come to guide them across the divide. These next two stories inspire me every time I read them:

> My dad was at home receiving hospice care, in and out of a coma for three days before he passed away. On the second day, he came out of his coma, but seemed to be unaware of his surroundings. He kept looking up at the corner of the room and reaching his arms out as if trying to hug someone. He put his hands together as if praying. He then straightened the oxygen tubing under his chin and fumbled around with his fingers from the top of his breastbone to the end of it.
>
> He died the next day, and when the hospice nurse came over, we asked her about it. She said she had seen this before and it was not unusual. She said he was getting dressed to leave. Straightening the oxygen tube under his chin represented straightening out his tie, and the finger movements along his breastbone was buttoning up his shirt. It made complete sense because that is exactly what it looked like he was doing.
>
> —NANCY, CHATTANOOGA, TN

My mother was born in 1924 and her brother was born a few years before her. I don't know exactly the year. But when he was a little two-year-old baby, he caught scarlet fever and he was dying. His mother was rocking him on the front porch when suddenly he reached both his arms up, as if to be held by someone (there was no one there) and said, "Mama, the angels are here for me." At that moment he died in her arms.[2]

Even more common are reports from people who are dying seeing something or talking to someone not visible to the others in the room. They often see the beauty of heaven, a mother or mother figure, siblings, or people who weren't yet known to have died. They often talk about getting ready for a trip, ask about their luggage or tickets, describe angels, or mention the name of the person who is coming to get them.

Steve Jobs, the founder and CEO of Apple Computing, was recognized worldwide as a pioneer of the personal computer revolution and was sometimes referred to as a genius. Although a person of exceptional intelligence, vision, and drive, he was typical of so many other people: He was taken to Sunday school as a child but, at age thirteen, his response to seeing a photo of starving children in Biafra was to turn away from a God who would allow such suffering. Many people believe he later became a Buddhist, but toward the end of his life, he said, "I'm kind of 50/50 on believing in God." He wanted something to endure but acknowledged it might just be wishful thinking. In his final moments, he stared past his loving family and proclaimed, "Oh wow, oh wow, oh wow."[3]

I keep wondering, *What or whom did this brilliant man see that sparked such wonder?*

In 2012, my brother-in-law died of a rare brain infection.

He was an extremely smart, quick-witted, and articulate man, but during the week prior to his death, his mental clarity waxed and waned. He was not a spiritual or religious man, but during more than one of his lucid phases when I was sitting at his bedside, he explained that he felt "trapped between the worlds." He said he was going back and forth between our world and God's world, and that he was speaking with angels. He asked if I could see them. He asked my sister to make sure their children knew Jesus.

Stories of deathbed visions (DBVs) are even more common than near-death experiences and, similar to NDEs, have been described since antiquity. A DBV often gives a dying person a glimpse of deceased loved ones. Or angels appear to help them make their transition to the next world. These DBVs occur in the days, hours, or moments before death. I have read estimates that one-half to two-thirds of dying people report experiencing DBVs.[4, 5, 6]

Remarkably, people in the same room or even at a distance can occasionally share in these end-of-life visions.

Similar to NDEs, deathbed visions often include people who have already died, even if the experiencer does not yet know the person to be dead. An example of this was reported by William Barrett:

Lady Barrett, an obstetrical surgeon in Dublin, delivered a healthy child to Doris (her last name was withheld from the written report), but Doris was dying of a hemorrhage. As the doctors waited next to the dying woman, she began to see things.

As Lady Barrett tells it, "Suddenly she looked eagerly toward part of the room, a radiant smile illuminating her whole countenance. 'Oh, lovely, lovely,' she said. I asked, 'What is lovely?' 'What I see,' she replied in low, intense tones. 'What do you see?' 'Lovely brightness—wonderful beings.' It is dif-

ficult to describe the sense of reality conveyed by her intense absorption in the vision. Then—seeming to focus her attention more intently on one place for a moment—she exclaimed, almost with a kind of joyous cry: 'Why, it's father! He's so glad I'm coming. He's so glad.' She spoke to her father, saying, 'I am coming,' then looked at me. When she looked at that same place again, she said, with a rather puzzled expression, 'He has Vida with him.' She turned to me and repeated, 'Vida is with him.' She then said, 'You do want me, Dad; I am coming.'

"Then she died. The sister of Doris, Vida, had died three weeks earlier, but since Doris was in such delicate condition, the death of her beloved sister was kept a secret from her."[7]

Another story about a shared DBV came to me from Katie:

When my fiancé was minutes from his death, I sat beside his bed and reassured him that it was okay to let go and go to God. I let him know that I am a strong woman and that I would be all right. When I finished talking, he opened his eyes and looked deeply into my eyes. His eyes were shining with a light that came through them. We were both encased in some sort of a bubble that was not of this earth. I felt a very deep joy, love, happiness, and peace that we as humans cannot imagine. It was so intense, so beautiful. It seemed he spoke to me through his mind. One of the things he said was that it all makes sense in the end.

This experience lasted approximately fifteen seconds. I was slowly taken back to myself and at that same moment, he slowly closed his eyes, let out a breath, and died.

This was a very powerful experience. I feel blessed that this happened to me. I will never have any doubts that there is an afterlife that is peaceful. He died four years ago and came to

me one time. I don't care if anyone believes this or not. I do
know that there is life after death and that we are protected and
watched over by our loved ones.

—Katie, McLean, VA

VISITS FROM BEYOND

Katie's story also mentions that her fiancé came to her once after his death. This is quite frequently reported, and I have been asked many times whether I have "spoken" with my son since his death. On three occasions, I have had "dreams" in which Willie was present. I call them dreams but like so many other people who have shared their stories of nighttime visitations, I believe my son's spirit was actually present.

In the first visitation, my son and I just held each other while he told me he was fine. I could feel him and hear him. I'm not sure I could smell him, but I was able to take in his very essence.

In the second visitation, I happily watched as he and his siblings lightheartedly played together on a swing set. I awoke with a deep longing to have my son for just one more day. This experience was so distressing that I never wanted another visitation.

Several months later, however, Willie came again. God's pervasive love filled the space as he and I stood together under a light pole in the dark of the universe. It is difficult to describe, but eventually I was asked to voluntarily relinquish his spirit. He pointed to where he lived and with heartbreaking compassion said, "I live there now." I knew Willie was where he belonged, and I knew that we both had work to do, his in heaven and mine on Earth. I also knew that life on Earth is just a blink of time, and I was confident that Willie would be the first to greet me when my work on Earth is done.

Despite this knowledge, relinquishing his spirit was the most difficult thing I have ever been asked to do. I gathered him in my arms, smothered him in my tears, and then lifted him up to the heavens. He was gone, and I knew I would not see him again during my physical life.

Similar to the times when God directs angels to cross into our world, the people, or spirits, who come during a "dream visitation" seem to be sent with a purpose. The visit is never from someone who is still alive, and the person or animal in the visitation always appears healthy, relaxed, and at peace. They are whole and complete. The visitor is always loving, and without anger or disappointment during the visit, regardless of his or her relationship with the experiencer during life.

Stories from the Cokeville, Wyoming, elementary school bombing in May 1986 may also show that, in addition to angelic visits, our deceased loved ones may be able to offer us help in times of need. Jennie Sorensen, who was a first-grader at the time of the Cokeville bombing, recounts:

The whole afternoon was a large miracle encompassed with lots of smaller miracles, but a few miracles that I personally witnessed have been difficult over the years for me to share publicly. I reserved sharing anything for twenty years, besides with my immediate family and at very safe functions, because of potential ridicule from others. There was one very personal miracle for me that day. I had a "teacher" I did not know help me out of that burning classroom. I never said anything to anyone until we were looking through family albums for my grandma when I was eleven or twelve. When I saw one photo, I asked what grade this particular woman in the photo had taught and why she quit teaching after the bomb. My grandma looked at the picture of her aunt I was referring to and said she had never been a teacher that she knew of and not in Cokeville.

I continued to explain that she was the teacher who led me out when the bomb went off. With tears in her eyes, she explained to me that there is no way she could have been there because she had died earlier in the 1980s. She also told me that she was extremely close to this aunt. I knew she was there and saved me. I didn't see angels in white, but I saw and listened to who I needed to.[8]

There are no distractions during the dream visit, which is always logical and sequential, and the message—usually one of comfort and reassurance, even when containing a warning—is clearly and unmistakably conveyed before the person, or spirit, quickly departs. The experiencer typically awakens with a profound sense of peace and love, and, as with NDEs or other out-of-body events, the memory of a dream visitation never fades.

In 1997, I was eight months pregnant with my first and only child. I was thirty-eight years old and single. I had lost my mother and best friend fourteen years earlier. I visited with my gynecologist on a Monday, and all looked good and right on schedule to deliver the baby in four weeks.

I went to bed that evening and woke up a little after midnight. I had had the most incredible dream! I dreamt that my mom and I were holding hands and walking on the beach, just as we had done many times when I was growing up. She looked angelic, peaceful, and beautiful. I couldn't stop looking at her in my dream.

She told me, "Ginger, you are going to have the baby today." I told her, no, not today. The doctor just told me four more weeks. Mom looked at me again and repeated, "You are going to have the baby today." As I lay there in bed, I could not stop thinking about how very real this dream was. In the years

*since she had passed, I had never had such a feeling of physical
closeness with her.*

*I went to use the bathroom and then back to bed. But I was
unable to sleep since I was so excited about this dream. And
that's when my water broke! I did indeed have the baby that
same day.*

*There is no one in this world who could tell me this was only
a dream. For me, I know it was a visitation from my mom.*

—Ginger, Albuquerque, NM

I must admit that I would have been rather dismissive of
this sort of phenomenon if I had not experienced it myself.
As much as I try to mitigate it, and as much as it seems like I
should easily embrace spiritual matters, it is in my nature to
be a persistent "doubting Thomas." I sympathize with people
who assume these sorts of dream visitations are nothing more
than an expression of the dreamer's unconscious desire. Remarkably, however, the content of these visitations is rarely
what the dreamer would hope for and the experiencer never
doubts the reality of the visitation. In the case of those who
are dying, out-of-body visitors and heavenly messages un-
questionably ease the departing one's fears. But overwhelmingly, their purpose is simple and profound: to reassure people
at their most vulnerable time that they are deeply, personally,
and everlastingly loved by God.

NO PAIN IN PASSING ON

I accept that I may not ever know the answers for all the
"whys" of my son's death, but I have absolute confidence that
there continues to be incredible hope and beauty that has
come from his life, as well as from his death.

Many people are haunted by the assumption that someone

who died violently or traumatically must have suffered greatly. It should be comforting to know that, based on my own experience with death and thousands of other NDE stories, I am confident that no one has pain at the time of his or her passing, regardless of how it appears to those of us still in the physical world. I believe the dying person's spirit is often welcomed home by God's messengers before the body has actually died. In fact, my own definition of death has actually changed as a result of my experience: Rather than it being the point at which a physical body has irrevocably and completely ceased to exhibit life, I define death as the point at which one's spirit permanently leaves its physical body.

THE SECOND LESSON THAT HEAVEN REVEALS

Death is not to be feared, because death is not the end.
It is a threshold where we leave our physical selves
behind and walk whole into eternity.

I had absolutely no fear or pain as I was drowning, as my legs were breaking, as I was being resuscitated, or as I was being transported for treatment. A similar lack of pain or fear has been shared with me by many, many other people who also returned from a state of near death. Despite my lack of discomfort as I was resuscitated and transported, I made sounds that other people assumed indicated agonizing pain. My companions later told me I had made "unearthly" noises and groaning. I may have been in emotional agony because I didn't want to return to my body, but I was definitely not in physical agony.

Even as Willie's body was broken, I am certain he did not suffer, was greeted by God's most gentle messengers, and had been reassured that his loved ones on Earth would be fine. I am also pretty sure that he would not have returned to Earth if given the choice.

Even when a death is not sudden or traumatic, all suffering seems to disappear prior to physical death. This phenomenon is frequently reported by hospice nurses and family members, who routinely describe seeing expressions of calm, peace, and wonder that overcome people as they reach the end of life.

SEEING THROUGH TO THE OTHER SIDE

Which brings me to my biggest personal awakening as a trained practitioner in the health sciences after my NDE.

Death is not to be feared because death is not the end.

Of course, as a spinal surgeon, I'd been around death in my education, training, and practice for years, but I had yet to personally suffer the loss of a loved one. What's more, I had never really considered my own death. Other than believing in a god, and thinking there was probably "something more" after death, I had no expectations or preconceptions about what death would be like.

The experiences I am telling you about in this book changed all that, and not in a theoretical way. To realize that death is really *not* the end has radically changed my perception of what life means in very practical ways—how I feel about God, what I hope for, believe in, and expect—and I know this truth can do the same for you.

Chapter 4

SITTING NEXT TO JESUS

"God loves us because of who God is, not because of who we are. That is grace."

—Philip Yancey

After an out-of-body experience, some have described the difficulty of reentering their body—a resistance or confusion that can be almost comical. But my reentry was simple and gentle. I merely sat down on top of my body, stretched out my legs, and lay backward into my torso. With that, I reunited with the physical world.

I opened my eyes and looked into the faces of my friends. There, I not only saw exhilaration, surprise, and shock, but also fear and apprehension. Against all statistical odds, they had revived a dead person who was now significantly injured and lying on the bank of an inaccessible river in a remote part of a distant country.

What now?

To find medical attention, our group faced enormous obstacles. For starters, we had no cell phones, radios, or other means of communication—remember that all this occurred before cell phones and cell towers became so commonplace.

And even if there had been a means of communication, there were no emergency service providers with whom to communicate. Although much has changed since then, at the time of these events, we were kayaking in a remote and undeveloped part of Chile that was far from any sort of hospital, and even farther from one that would provide ambulance service.

And then there was my husband. The team didn't know where he was and had no way to contact him.

Suddenly, circumstances changed. Two Chilean men materialized on the riverbank next to our group. Where had they come from? How did they know we were in trouble? There was no way to access this part of the river without a boat, and these men had no boat or any other means of transportation. Seemingly out of nowhere, they were just standing there!

Without speaking or being spoken to, the two men walked over and helped lift my body onto a kayak. Using the kayak as a stretcher, they, along with my friends, began to knock down the thick bamboo to make a trail so they could move me up the steep hillside.

After what seemed like endless bushwhacking, our group finally emerged onto a dirt road. As I was carried up and out of the foliage, we immediately encountered an ambulance parked on the side of the road. It seemed to be waiting for us.

Just as the men on the riverbank had said nothing, the driver of the ambulance, who did not seem surprised to see us, asked no questions about the situation or about what happened. He simply and very calmly moved into action.

Let me repeat this. With no communications and no hospitals anywhere nearby, two men "just happened" to appear on the riverbank to help us find a way out. They led my boat mates directly to an ambulance that "just happened" to be waiting with a driver at the exact time and place of our appearance on an infrequently traveled dirt road in a remote part of South America.

And, just as astonishingly, my husband, Bill, and another kayaker were also there. Apparently, the American kayaker who had panicked and run during my resuscitation had unintentionally—and seemingly randomly—come upon the spot where my husband had been reading. Together, they drove on the road leading downriver, reaching the spot where we emerged onto the road *at the very moment* we emerged. Had they arrived at this point in the road a few minutes earlier, or later, they would have seen nothing and passed on by.

As Bill and I made our journey back to the United States, and for a couple of weeks afterward, I inexplicably experienced no physical pain. This was despite having suffered multiple broken bones and torn ligaments in and about my knees. No pain whatsoever. On a ten-point scale, zero.

Later I wondered if my recollections were inaccurate, but such was not the case. I thoroughly reviewed all my medical records, confirming that I had not received any sort of medication that could have created this sense of painlessness or well-being. I also received nothing that would have been psychotropic, with the ability to alter my mental state or cause hallucinations.

Which is important because of what I will tell you next.

GRACE HAS A FACE, AND A NAME

While I was in the hospital care units in Jackson, I had two more out-of-body experiences. In each, I returned to heaven.

One experience was brief, but it allowed me, once again, to feel that overwhelming sense of being totally and unreservedly loved by an awesome and supernatural God.

The second was longer and more involved. I sat on the ground at one end of a long field. The field was filled with wild grasses gently swaying in a soft breeze. The entire area was bathed in the beautiful, golden glow of a late-afternoon sun. My arms rested comfortably on top of my knees. The ground beneath felt firm. The world around me glimmered with . . . what? Exhilaration! Yes, that's what seemed to fill creation.

As with my earlier experiences, these struck me as being more real than real. Colors were more intense than those found on Earth. Smells and sounds effortlessly filled my consciousness, and God's pure love infused everything. The edges of the field expanded into the universe, with no apparent beginning or end. I could see people joyfully twirling and playing at the far end of the field, although I could not tell if they were children or adults.

Yet one person, who was sitting on the rock next to me, was utterly, inarguably known to me.

He was Jesus.

I have been asked how I knew it was Jesus with whom I was having a conversation in this sun-drenched field. Some people have assumed that I just imagined it because I wanted it to be Jesus. Others have tried to convince me that the one I took to be a person with a name was really just a collection of energy—the Source of all love.

But I had no doubt it was Jesus and didn't need to ask his name. Asking would be like seeing my husband in the grocery store and, before starting a conversation, asking, "Are you Bill?" Absurd. I knew it was Jesus in the same way that I knew everything else in my experience—with a pure, deep, and absolute understanding. I didn't just *wish* it were Jesus, *hope* it was Jesus, or *think* it was. I *knew* it was Jesus.

Of course, I have also often been asked what Jesus looked

like. My answer is both simple and complex. He looked like endless kindness and compassion. Period. I realize that *kindness* and *compassion* are not words we use to describe visual attributes, but that is truly what He "looked" like to me in those moments. Other words just wouldn't communicate what I saw. He seemed to intimately know both the pain and joy of this world, its beauty and its ugliness. He absorbed all of it and covered it with His love.

As for the color of His eyes, skin, and hair, I would say that they encompassed the essence of all colors. I know—not helpful if you're trying to narrow things down to a particular hue. Yet, when you look around at the world, maybe it makes sense. If twenty people were put in a room and examined, no two people would have exactly the same eye, skin, or hair colors. We are all reflections of God. (In the Bible, Jesus told his followers, "He who has seen me has seen the Father.") The closest I am able to get when describing this is to go back to my description of the multitude of colors I saw and experienced when I traveled the path just after my death. Just as I cannot precisely describe, in isolation, any single color along that path, I cannot settle on any one single visual description of Jesus's hair, eyes, skin, or other attributes. Human language, at least for me, isn't up to the task.

While we talked, I asked Jesus a lot of questions, although I'm unable to recall many of them now. In reply, I felt that I was receiving a complete understanding of the divine order of the universe and our interconnectedness. Everything struck me as logical, interwoven, and magnificent.

What I'll never forget was that, during the whole conversation, Jesus was endlessly patient, gentle, and mesmerizing. He seemed light of spirit, with a sense of humor.

I could not take my attention off of Him. And I didn't want to. I never wanted to be anywhere else except in his presence.

TREMBLING IN THE PRESENCE

When I wrote my first book, I referred to this presence rather vaguely, I'll admit. There, I called Him an "angel, messenger, Christ, or teacher." But why didn't I share the true identity of the man next to me? I *did* know who He was, and without a doubt.

Thinking about it in the years since, I've realized that part of me wanted to keep this most private aspect of my experience just for myself. For some reason, I just didn't want to share everything, fearing that revealing it would make it less special. I have since discovered that this is a common concern for others who have had a deeply emotional or spiritual experience.

But something else held me back. Truthfully, I wasn't ready to confess what I knew to be true because I knew there was nothing I had ever done to earn the right to have a conversation with Jesus.

Of course, I can never earn the *right* to speak with Jesus, nor can I ever be "good enough" to bask in His love for me. But, oh how I wanted to! I wanted to deserve it.

If you're like me, receiving something wonderful that you *know* you didn't earn can be hard to swallow. It certainly runs counter to our risk-and-reward, crime-and-punishment culture. If we succeed at work, we expect to receive the accolades, and hopefully the bonus. That's only fair, right? If our children turn out well, we're pretty sure it's because of our good parenting. If we believe the right things, and live a "good" life, we're pretty sure our prayers will get answered the way we want.

A mean reverse logic also lurks in our hearts and minds. When things don't turn out well, we feel overlooked or punished by God. An inner voice cries out, *But I've tried to live a good life! Why did things turn out this way?*

Or we strongly object on someone else's behalf: *What did my kindhearted friend do to deserve cancer?*

Something's wrong with this picture. God does not play favorites, and none of us has earned what we receive—neither the perceived blessings nor the perceived troubles. It was Job, the Bible's poster child for suffering and unfair treatment, who said, "[God] shows no partiality to princes, and does not favor the rich over the poor, for they are all the work of his hands" (34:19).

Still, there's a ledger keeper in all of us. For some of us, the ledger only tracks the "good stuff." For others, it fixates on a long list of bad things, which we then hold over our own heads. Either way, the arithmetic is just as broken.

Thankfully, Jesus came to show another way. You and I don't have to "earn" an intimate moment with God. I didn't have to "deserve" a seat next to Jesus in that beautiful field. And I'm not required to earn his favor in order to spend an eternity enjoying God's love.

I know that now.

FREEDOM IN FORGIVENESS

It is truly good news that neither you nor I need to earn our way into God's family or into His loving embrace. When we make poor choices or ignore God's leading, He does not cast us away and forget about us. He continues to love us and patiently awaits our return. Regardless of who we are, where we are, or how many mistakes we have made, God will run to us when we turn toward Him. (For the picture of this that Jesus described, read his story about the prodigal son's return in Luke 15. Read more in John 12:32 and 1 Timothy 4:10.) When our failings run deep, God's love runs deeper.

He knows our story. He understands our heart and knows

our hurts. In fact, He knew us before we were in our mother's womb (Jeremiah 1:5). He looks beyond our outward appearance, seeing our beauty and promising to remove our mistakes as far as the east is from the west (Psalm 103:12). Instead of focusing on our shortcomings, God focuses on our potential. As Oscar Wilde observed, "Every saint has a past, and every sinner has a future."

As we release our story to God, we can let go of our past failures (Isaiah 43:18–19), shame, guilt, anger, and disappointments. And through His forgiveness, we have the ability to live a future that is not defined by our past. With God, every new day is another blank page of our life's book just waiting to be filled.

Recognizing our own failings and accepting God's forgiveness of them makes it easier to show grace to those who we don't think "deserve" forgiveness—perhaps we don't think they have shown adequate remorse, don't understand the pain they caused, or haven't suffered deeply enough. We may even feel virtuous in our withholding of forgiveness, as did a woman I recently read about.

When she was asked about forgiveness during her lecture on Anne Frank, she stated that she does "not hold the Holocaust against the Germans, but that she would never forgive the Nazis for what they did." She stated that, being Jewish, she would "never abandon her people like that."

Many people felt a righteous anger when Nelson Mandela called for reconciliation rather than revenge after his release from twenty-seven years of imprisonment and torture.

The choice to hang on to bitterness and anger may feel virtuous but has a destructive nature. As the wise theologian Lewis Smedes said, "When we attach our feelings to the moment when we were hurt, we endow it with immortality. And we let it assault us every time it comes to mind. It travels with us, sleeps with us, hovers over us while we make love, and broods over us while we die. Our hate does not even have the decency to die when those we hate die—for it is a parasite sucking *our* blood, not theirs. There is only one remedy for it; forgiveness."[1]

I recently read about an exercise that emphasizes this point. Fill a glass or jar with water. Pick it up and hold it in front of you, at arm's length. Simple, right? Keep holding it straight out in front of you. Pretty soon you will feel the muscles in your arm tire, and then your arm will begin to shake with fatigue. Eventually, your arm will drop from the weight of the water-filled glass that you first thought was so light.

Refusing to forgive may seem like an insignificant burden, but its emotional weight will slowly crush us if we fail to let it go. It keeps us in bondage to our past. It gives past events the power to define us, often limiting where we go, what we do, and the space available for love.

When we choose to forgive, we choose to accept the depth of God's love and grace for all people, acknowledging that there is some good in the worst of us and some evil in the best of us. It concedes that we cannot see the bigger picture of God's intricate tapestry of life.

THE THIRD LESSON THAT HEAVEN REVEALS

Choosing forgiveness releases our burdens and frees us to live fully and joyfully in God's extravagant love.

And that is the incredible wonder of it all. God bathes you and me in His pure love *because God is love.* He rejoices over us with singing (Zephaniah 3:17). You see, whether we believe it or not, whether we live like it or not, God's love is an unshakable reality. He covers you and me completely with mercy because His name is mercy, and His nature is Grace, and you and I and every other person who has ever lived are His beloved children. God promises that when you choose to accept His love, you will experience life more fully and more abundantly than you ever thought possible.

Too soon, Jesus gave me a gentle kiss on top of my head, our conversation ended, and I was once again beneath the covers of my bed in the hospital. I sensed that I was back to stay—that the veil between this world and the next, so recently transparent, was beginning to thicken and conceal. My spirit and body would probably remain joined until my death. And the next steps of my journey would again be on solid ground.

Chapter 5

LIFE GOES FURTHER THAN SCIENCE

"An error does not become truth by reason of multiplied propagation, nor does truth become error because nobody sees it."

—Mahatma Gandhi

In the days and weeks after I drowned, I felt like I was neither here nor there. I had one foot on Earth and one foot in heaven. Part of me was deeply disappointed to be back—heaven had been so intense and complete. By comparison, the life I returned to seemed like a faded black-and-white copy of the brilliantly colorful original.

There were physical aftereffects, too. When I had arrived in the ICU back in the States, my vision was blurred, and I found myself unable to focus on anything for more than one or two seconds. I wasn't able to watch television, read books, or even hold a conversation. It was easier to just keep my eyes closed.

After a couple of days, I asked for a bible only to discover that I couldn't manage reading even familiar passages. Then, just as I started to set the Bible aside in frustration, two words jumped from the page: "Rejoice always" (1 Thessalonians 5:16). Later, words from the following verses in the same chapter also became clear: "Pray without ceasing" (5:17 ESV) and "Give thanks in all circumstances, for this is the will of God in Christ Jesus for you" (5:18 ESV). Everything else, and all other reading material, remained blurry for several more days.

I have since wondered if my inability to focus was a little bit of brain injury from my being without oxygen for so long. But that certainly wouldn't explain why my vision was *selectively* clear. With no logical or physiologic explanation for how this could happen, I took it as yet another in a long sequence of miracles.

As you'd expect, I spent a lot of time during my recovery trying to figure things out.

Given what I already knew about cardiopulmonary resuscitation (CPR), I first wondered how I could possibly have survived. The generally held belief that CPR works well is most likely the result of popular television shows, which depict a 75 percent success rate. Despite becoming a routine part of medical care since its introduction in 1960, I knew the outcomes in real life are significantly different, with only a 2 percent likelihood of survival for people who collapse on the street and receive CPR before arrival at a hospital,[1, 2, 3]— and that number doesn't even include people who were pronounced dead on the scene and, therefore, never taken to the hospital. The statistical likelihood of survival becomes zero after eight minutes of no treatment, or twelve minutes if CPR is included.

Survival after thirty minutes, which is how long my resuscitators believe I was without oxygen before CPR was initiated, is out of the question.

As I've described for you, we were in a remote area, nowhere near advanced medical care, and there were no mitigating factors. Some say I must have been trapped within an air pocket, and since I had been a "scientific-minded skeptic" about spiritual encounters, this was one of my own initial assumptions. I even considered whether my helmet could have created a small pocket of air by holding my head off the deck of my boat.

Before I lost consciousness underwater, however, I did multiple self-assessment examinations and considered that very question. After the drowning occurred, I became simultaneously aware of what was happening to my spiritual self and to my physical self. Even while being held by Christ, a part of my brain, or consciousness, was able to objectively assess what was happening. This part of my consciousness, while astounded at what was unfolding, never lost my analytical nature and continually questioned the reality of what was going on. I intermittently questioned how I felt, if I was still aware of my circumstances, if I could feel my boat and the water, if I was breathing or making any other movements, if I could hear or physically feel anything, and if I was afraid. I was curious about my fear, as I had always thought drowning would be a particularly frightening way to die.

Each time I took a moment to focus on the sensations of my mouth, nose, and chest, I felt no air movement. At one point, I noticed the sensation of my chest forcibly expanding, but feeling only water. For a moment, I imagined myself as a fish or a fetus, silently moving fluid in and out of my lungs. I felt like a leaf being pressed between the pages of a scrapbook as the weight of the water pressed my face against the rough plastic of my boat. My helmet, which had been ripped from my head by the force of the current, clearly did not create an air pocket.

Given the circumstances and my submersion time, my predicted survival rate was zero, and to imagine my surviving without severe brain injury would have been laughable.

I had so many questions and I knew I needed to try to figure out what actually happened to me, beginning with, Was my experience real and, if so, what did it all mean? I had almost no framework for understanding or describing any of it, but the scientist in me just couldn't tolerate not coming up with a clear, convincing, and medically credible explanation. I wanted to know exactly what occurs in the human body during and after drowning. I wanted to know how I could survive thirty minutes without oxygen and have no noticeable consequences when, in everyday life, I can barely hold my breath for one minute. I needed to understand my out-of-body experiences.

Like most people who have an NDE, I knew one thing with utter, unwavering certainty—something profound and extraordinary and wonderful *had* happened. And what's more, I felt like a different person. Life back on Earth felt different, too.

Still, I knew I would not be able to pick up the pieces and return to my everyday life until I understood everything and could explain it all, at least to myself. But I knew I needed to be methodical in my search for answers. After all the trauma I had sustained, could I trust my cognitive ability to help me reach reliable conclusions?

Fortunately, my vision and thinking skills quickly made a full recovery. As soon as I had the stamina to do it, I began my search—at first slowly, but then with increasing focus. This chapter is the story of that quest—part survivor story, part medical sleuthing, and all incredibly important for beginning a conversation about NDEs that is grounded in facts. For some, the science-focused content of this chapter may seem daunting, even unnecessary. For others, it will be the single most important chapter in the book.

WHAT JUST HAPPENED?

At the time of my NDE, I felt alone in my experience. Now, of course, I know that many, many people have had NDEs, and that profound commonalities mark our experiences. But back then, I didn't know. I didn't even know what the term meant. Early on in my search, I might have been persuaded to agree with the blogger who, in May 2013, wrote in response to Ben Breedlove's online sharing of his NDE: "While I truly believe Breedlove saw those bright lights and felt that deep sense of calm, I don't believe that what he saw and felt were 'evidence' of another realm. Rather, they were the dreams and hallucinations so often brought on by brain malfunctions, powerful drugs, and our own rich imaginations in the midst of life-threatening illness or trauma."[4]

The blogger supported her position by describing an allergic reaction she had had to peanuts in which she "experienced an extreme sense of calm" and a vision of her own funeral from beneath a table. She wrote that she did not see angels, bright lights, tunnels, or staircases to heaven. In her view, NDEs are "colored entirely by our own unique backgrounds, philosophies, personalities, and values." She concluded, "When faced with our own mortality, Breedlove and I both imagined what comes after death. He's religious; I'm not. He saw an after-life. I saw a funeral."[5]

Another blogger concluded his discussion of NDEs by writing, "Therefore, whatever at your deepest core you expect to happen when you die. . . . Congratulations, that's what'll happen. . . . Every religion was right."[6]

While these opinions may be interesting, they were not helpful to me in trying to understand my own experience. I really hadn't had any expectations about what death would be like or what would happen afterward. As such, how could my subconscious have created either the scope or the details of my experience? As a spinal surgeon, I'd been around death in my education, training, and practice but had yet to personally suffer the loss of a loved one. What's more, I had never really considered my own death. Other than saying that I believed in a God, and thinking there was probably "something more" after death, I had no preconceptions about what death would be like, and really didn't give it any thought.

Besides, as my family and coworkers could tell you, I have always seemed to be missing the imagination gene. A friend who has known me for twenty years told another friend that what I had written in my first book "must be true" because he "knew me to have no creative ability whatsoever." He didn't mean it as a criticism, but merely an observation that compelled him to both read my account and reconsider his own views on death after doing so.

Rather than accepting the cynical, dismissive, and anecdotal conclusions of people like the bloggers I mentioned, I wanted to systematically evaluate as much data as possible before forming conclusions. Understanding the nature of my experience was of paramount importance to me, and not just for clinical reasons. This was personal, I'll admit, but perhaps not in the way you might expect. A huge part of me desperately wanted to find a reason to *not* believe the reality or details of my experience and, therefore, to *not* believe the things I had been told. Finding a reasonable explanation would allow me to return to the ordinary life I had known. It would allow me to forget what I had been told about my son's future. I certainly did not want to face the challenges that had been set before me and did not relish the idea of sharing my experiences with others.

In any case, I pressed on. As a first step, I "came out" to one of my medical partners about my experiences because I thought he would listen rationally and critically. He listened intently as I spoke but then began to cry. He told me he was crying out of envy. This was definitely not the reaction I expected, and his response made me less inclined to share my experience with anyone else. I never even told the entire "story" to my husband. He was already so overwhelmed with the heroic task of caring for me, our young children, and running our medical practices that I didn't want to add to his burdens. For many months, perhaps years, he was also filled with terror at having almost lost me and consumed with guilt for not having protected me.

So instead of talking more, I kept my head down and stuck to my research, beginning with what happened at the river.

DID I ACTUALLY DROWN?

I pored over my medical records, spoke with the people who had been at the river and with those who received me into the emergency room, and I tried to corroborate as many details as possible. I read a great deal about drowning, the physiology of a dying brain, and the phenomenon of NDEs.

I knew there had been no air pocket, aerated water, or other source of oxygen to readily explain my survival, so I first considered whether a mammalian diving reflex could have been responsible. This survival reflex, which is triggered when very cold water splashes the face of aquatic mammals, and diving birds, causes the heart rate to slow and can initiate a redistribution of blood, sending more of it to the brain and heart. This physiologic response decreases the oxygen requirements of these animals, allowing them to spend a greater length of time under the water. In my experience, this "cold water reflex" seems to be the "go-to" explanation given when people try to explain survival after prolonged drowning.

I was no different in my assumptions, and thought this reflex might explain both my survival and lack of neurologic impairment. The problem I encountered is that the actual data did not support this conclusion.

This generally held belief that water temperature makes a significant difference for most drowning victims is basically an urban legend that arose after a somewhat cursory 1987 study observed a small neurological benefit that occurred in young children, with little body fat, who underwent very rapid cooling in water temperatures of less than 5 degrees Celsius (40 degrees Fahrenheit). Although it might seem like stories of toddlers being revived after falling into an icy lake abound, there are actually few written reports. The 1987 study showed that even under these ideal conditions, when a child fell into an icy lake and almost immediately became hypothermic, 35 percent died and 33 percent had serious neurologic aftereffects.[7]

A more complete 2002 study from Dr. Suominen, et. al., in the departments of Anesthesia and Intensive Care at the Helsinki University Hospital for Children and Adolescents evaluated the effect of age, submersion time, water temperature, and emergency room body temperature on survival rates in cases of near drowning. Their data showed the only significant predictor of survival and neurologic disability was submersion time. Even with submersion times of less than ten minutes, fewer than 2 percent of people survived more than one month, regardless of age.[8] The conclusion that submersion time is the only significant predictor of outcome and that water temperature offered no significant protection to the drowning victim has been supported in more recent studies, including a comprehensive 2014 study done at the University of Washington.[9]

Even if I decided to completely ignore the data and conclusions of these scientists, and ignore the fact that I was neither young at the time of my drowning nor submerged in freezing water, the reflexive redistribution of blood that occurs in the diving reflex is meaningless if the blood sent contains no oxygen. The diving reflex does not change the basic physiologic process of anoxia—aquatic mammals cannot stay under the water indefinitely. The eventual absence of oxygen reaching vital organs leads to death—so even this grasped-for explanation was implausible. And it did nothing to explain what came next for me.

WAS IT JUST MY IMAGINATION?

Maybe my subsequent out-of-body experiences were just the result of being given some "really good" drugs while in the hospital. But my medical records showed that I didn't get any sort of medication, let alone ones that could cause hallucinations. Cardiologist Dr. Pim van Lommel's 2001 study showed that it would not have made a difference anyway, that the administration of medications had absolutely no influence on the likelihood of a person experiencing an NDE.[10]

I then wondered if my NDE was a subconscious creation resulting from a dream or stress-related hallucination. Both dreams and hallucinations typically deny reality, and most of us have experienced the fantastical creatures and impossible activities that often materialize within dreams. We have likely experienced the sensation of flying, time travel, talking animals, and sudden transformations of both people and objects. As Dr. Allan Hobson, a well-known dream researcher, writes, "Dreams are illogical in their content and organization, the unities of time, place, and person do not apply, and natural laws are disobeyed." He goes on to write that dream content is often mysterious and puzzling and rarely follows a logical sequence of events.[11]

This is in contrast to the typical NDE. There, as in my experience, events proceed in a logical and organized manner, even while there is a shift in time and dimension. Rarely does the content of NDEs seem strange or bizarre, despite most experiencers' recognition that they have left their body and are probably dead. Unlike a typical dream or hallucination, reality is also not distorted or denied in an NDE—it is just perceived as another reality superimposed on this one.

Hobson points out that dreams and hallucinations often contain intense emotions of anxiety, fear, and surprise. NDEs, on the other hand, are usually devoid of these emotions. In fact, experiencers typically describe feelings of intense peace, calm, and love. Despite the bizarre and fantastical elements of many of our dreams, if we can remember the experience, we can put it into words. But this is not typical of the otherworldly aspects of an NDE. Language simply comes up short. This is why the descriptions of near death and other spiritual experiences are so filled with analogies, similes, and metaphors.

Another hallmark of dreams, hallucinations, and delirium is that the details of these experiences are poorly recalled— and the further we get away from the event, the more the details fade. Ninety-five percent of all dreams are forgotten entirely upon awakening. Even when bits and pieces of a vivid dream are written down, details become only vaguely remembered over the course of hours and days and years.

One of the aspects of NDEs that I find truly fascinating is that the detailed memory of them simply never fades or changes. A not-uncommon testimonial goes like this: "That happened thirty years ago, but today the clarity of the experience remains as strong as the day it occurred."

WAS IT A SEIZURE?

But could my experience have been the result of a "short circuit" in my brain—for example, a combination of abnormal electrical signals or perhaps seizure activity?

At first, this line of questioning seemed more promising. Children who suffer from reflex anoxic seizures occasionally report feelings of flashes of light, smells, tastes, tunnels, sensations of floating or flying, distortions of body image, feelings of leaving one's body, or memories of events from the past. Specifically, however, these children never report beings of light, seeing deceased friends or relatives, angels, or pets, or any of the beautiful and inspiring scenes typically reported in childhood NDEs.[12, 13]

We know that whether naturally or surgically stimulated, the abnormal electrical stimulus of seizures certainly can cause people to have visual hallucinations, experience explosions of light, or have a feeling of being dissociated from their body.[14] Stimulation of a part of the right temporal lobe has reportedly produced visions of God, hearing beautiful music, and even seeing dead friends and relatives.

I wondered if all this could explain what Christians believe about the scriptures being God-breathed? What if the disciple Matthew merely had a seizure when he described an angel of the Lord as having an appearance like lightning and clothing as white as snow (Matthew 28:2–3)?

But this is a stretch and really doesn't make sense. While seizure-induced hallucinations can be vivid, the memories are always fragmented, nonsequential, never include elements that are unknowable to the experiencers, and have never produced the profound life reviews or transformational changes that are routinely observed in experiencers of NDEs.[15]

WAS IT OXYGEN DEPRIVATION?

Are you ready for a brief but illuminating Science of Drowning class? You might not consider yourself scientifically inclined in the slightest, but I encourage you to stay with me as I share with you the process and sequence of the body's response when its life-giving supply of oxygen is suddenly and completely shut off.

If you stay with me, despite the occasional unfamiliar word, I promise you'll never think about an NDE the same again.

Underwater and unable to breathe, my body's hungry use of the remaining oxygen within my bloodstream should have caused my carbon dioxide (CO_2) levels to rise. Yet I never felt the panic or intense sense of air hunger this would normally create.

Within a minute of my drowning, the amount of oxygen in my bloodstream would have dropped to almost zero. But although I may have *felt* like I was free of the need for oxygen, I definitely still needed it to keep my brain functioning. I should have lost consciousness, but that is not what happened. I only remember being conscious, followed by being *more* conscious.

Denying oxygen to the brain is like denying coal to a steam engine—it just isn't sustainable. A continuous supply of oxygen is needed by the human brain to convert glucose, a simple sugar, to adenosine triphosphate (ATP), and ATP is critical for the transfer of energy within cells for metabolism.

Think of it as the coal that provides the energy (heat) that converts water to steam, which is then harnessed to move the wheels of the train. So no coal means no heat means no steam. And without steam, even the mightiest steam engine is soon reduced to a silent, motionless collection of metal parts.

Similarly, the ATP generates the power needed to move electrically charged ions back and forth across cell membranes. This back-and-forth movement powered by ATP initiates the brain's release of more than a hundred known chemical messengers (neurotransmitters), which tell the rest of the body what to do. But without oxygen and glucose, there is no ATP. With no ATP, there is no power source. With no power, there is no brain activity. Lights out.

Within two to three minutes of my drowning, my laryngospasm (a reflexive closing of the back of the throat that typically occurs with drowning) would have released, causing an influx of water to my lungs. When my presumed laryngospasm released, and I felt the movement of water into my lungs, I felt inexplicably free. I imagined myself as a manta ray, which so beautifully and silently propels itself through the ocean depths.

This inhaled river water in my lungs would have caused hemolysis (a bursting open of the red blood cells), further increasing the potassium level in my bloodstream. In turn, this would have altered the electrical activity in my heart muscle, and in combination with increased acidosis from the accumulation of lactic acid and rising CO_2 levels, along with no signals from my brain, my heart would have stopped beating. Without a pump, blood would no longer even circulate through my vessels or within my brain.

Rebuttals to the NDE phenomenon often vaguely refer to a presumed residual activity in the brain's cortex, but they offer no explanation as to how this activity might be powered. This explanation requires a suspension of logic, and the rejection of the well-documented physiological processes I've just described.

Think about the implications of that for a moment: Wouldn't it be nonsensical to believe that a brain with no power, no electrical activity, and no function can independently form new, lucid, and complex memories that are precisely remembered for a lifetime?

One description of an NDE memory after drowning that struck me as quite representative came from Dr. Pim van Lommel's book *Consciousness Beyond Life:*

> *I had an NDE when I "drowned" at the age of five. I am now nearly eighty-two. Suddenly, an unspeakably beautiful spectrum of light surrounded me. It was wrapped by a most peaceful loving presence, remaining unchanging for a "long time" before I returned to earthly reality with a terrible thud and then heard excited human voices and a banging on my body. Today the clarity of the experience remains as strong as the day it occurred. Consciousness does survive death in all probability. I am an anesthesiologist.*[16]

Predictably and quickly, death ensues when no oxygen is forthcoming. It's accurate to describe death as a process as well as an event. So, to find the answers we're looking for, I want to further describe what happened during my process of dying (or anyone's, for that matter) in slow motion.

With no oxygen supply, no power to keep the cell membranes charged, and no circulation, there would be no energy to keep the neurons (nerve cells) in my brain polarized (just as it takes effort to keep two magnets away from each other, it takes energy to keep differently charged chemicals on different sides of a cell membrane). Without continued polarization of the membrane, my neurons would have uncontrollably dumped their neurotransmitters directly into my brain's synaptic clefts. These synaptic clefts are the gaps between neurons—the gaps through which communication must travel.

Imagine two brothers (neurons) standing on each side of a river (the cleft). They want to communicate but are too far apart to directly talk, so they solve this problem by asking a friend (a neurotransmitter) to deliver messages back and forth by swimming across the river.

Now imagine the neurons (people) on each side of the river are from different countries and don't speak the same language. The people on one side of the river calmly give their messages to a multilingual swimmer (the neurotransmitter) who can translate their message for the people on the other side. Neurotransmitter dumping by depolarized membranes would be like all the people shouting and pushing their translators into the river at the same time. There would be system overload, complete chaos, and all communication would fail.

Still, many people hypothesize that it is precisely during this time of chaotic dumping that brain cells *might* be exposed to a concentrated bath of neurotransmitters like dopamine and/or, N, N-Dimethyltryptamine (DMT), thus creating near-death experiences.

Not only has this never actually been shown to occur, but the hypothesis of neurotransmitter dumping causing the NDE has serious limitations. To begin with, the uncontrolled depolarization of neurons that occurs with a brain's power failure releases neurotransmitters in a toxic concentration that *kills* brain cells. This sudden die-off is intensified by the calcium-induced bursting of brain cells that results in the added release of tissue-destroying free radicals.

Furthermore, the brain tissue most sensitive to this destruction are the cells located within the horseshoe-shaped hippocampus—the area of the brain most responsible for the formation of new memories, and a critical component of transforming short-term memories into long-term ones. Without the hippocampus, no new long-term memories can form. None. In the context of drowning, after approximately five minutes without oxygen, the cells of my hippocampus should have suffered irreversible damage.[17, 18, 19]

You can see where this logic leads: If the hippocampus is the region of the brain most sensitive to this cell destruction, and if the hippocampus is primarily responsible for memory creation and retention, then it is entirely illogical to credit the sudden dumping of neurotransmitters with the vivid and intense memories that are remembered for a lifetime by people who have had an NDE.

But I had more reading to do. Despite what I saw as an illogical connection, I needed to know more about the known effects of both dopamine and, especially, DMT—the neurotransmitters that were most frequently mentioned in the literature when discussing the presumed cause of NDEs.

WAS IT A DMT TRIP?

Are you still with me? If you are not fond of science, I know we're moving quickly through some tedious words and demanding ideas, but it is important to understand the sequence. But I don't want you to miss out on the conclusion to my personal research, and we're almost there. To tantalize you to keep reading, I will tell you that this final lap of my marathon research will deliver surprises like, well, dreaming rodents, a so-called "God particle," alien beings, and a man named Scott who slipped into his encounter with death during what must have been a very boring company meeting.

Who knew that science could be this much fun?

I soon discovered that high levels of dopamine within the brain can produce euphoria, increase the intensity and frequency of dreams, and is released in anoxic events. On the other hand, it has also been shown to rapidly cause irreversible brain damage, does not stimulate either auditory or visual hallucinations, and has never been associated with any of the features typical of an NDE. For these reasons, I shifted my focus from dopamine to DMT.[20, 21]

I learned that DMT produces psychoactive effects when it is smoked, injected, or ingested. It is widely found in the plant world and has an affinity for both serotonin and dopamine receptor sites, neurotransmitters that both play a role in mood and feelings of pleasure.

There's a hitch, though: DMT has never actually been found in humans.

Still, because trace levels have been found in the pineal gland of rodents,[22] some researchers have proposed that increased concentrations of DMT *might* be present in humans and *might* be released from the human pineal gland at birth, during dream states, and at the time of death. They have even gone so far as to call DMT the "God particle."

Despite frequent mention of DMT and the fact that anecdotal accounts of DMT "journeys" populate the literature, no one has yet replicated psychiatrist Rick Strassman's groundbreaking work from the 1990s.

Between 1990 and 1995, Dr. Strassman administered four hundred doses of DMT to sixty healthy volunteers. In these studies, he observed that many of the volunteers had some combination of increased visual acuity and sense of color, feelings of being catapulted through space at incredibly high speeds, experiencing an all-encompassing glow, and a sense of unity and interconnectedness. Many felt a sense of enlightenment, and timelessness, and felt like they merged with a supremely powerful, wise, and loving presence. In this study, the DMT experiencers uniformly declared that consciousness continues after death of the body.

In his subsequent book *The Spirit Molecule,* Dr. Strassman describes this research experiment and suggests that *if* decomposing pineal tissue were to release DMT directly into the spinal fluid, it *might* reach the brain's sensory and emotional centers, causing residual awareness, and *might* explain the imagery reported by NDEers (emphasis is mine).[23] He went on to suggest that the human pineal gland *might* release DMT near the time of death, thereby accounting for the NDE phenomenon. Dr. Strassman's work has been used to imbue DMT with almost mythical qualities, and this is the most frequently used justification when dismissing the spiritual reality of NDEs.

Dr. Strassman's suggestions, however, were entirely speculative and have never been shown to be true. And then there's the fact that the DMT experience is qualitatively very different from that of an NDE.

The overwhelmingly constant feature of NDEs is that of intense, unconditional love from beings that are recognizable and engaging. This is in contrast to the elves, fairies, and other alien beings that those experiencing DMT encounter. These alien beings are unfamiliar, are often reptilian, insectoid, or complex robotic machines that can be hostile and uninterested in the experiencer.

Beyond the alien encounters, the DMT visual hallucinations typically involve seeing repeating colors in geometric patterns, described as "increasing geometry simply becoming so all-enveloping that absolutely nothing of the room is left anymore."[24] One DMT user wrote, "To the right of my mind space was a blue mass. [It was] a large entity formed of layers of strata, and bejeweled with many crystals along geometric fault lines which folded, twisted, and morphed its form in a mechanical fashion."[25]

According to Terence McKenna, with DMT, "the ordinary world is almost instantaneously replaced, not only with a hallucination, but a hallucination whose alien character is its utter alienness. Nothing in this world can prepare one for the impressions that fill your mind when you enter the DMT sensorium." *Yet,* as strange as many of the descriptions are of DMT experiences, psychedelic writer James Kent claims that a person can actually impose any imagery he or she wants when in the DMT state and can call these alien entities into existence.[26]

The consistently alien nature of a DMT experience, and one's ability to influence or control the experience, is in stark contrast to the entirely understandable visions and people described by those who have experienced near death.

DMT experiencers have also never reported veridical information—information received during the experience that coincides with real, but not yet known, events. And the memory of a DMT experience fades so quickly that proponents of using DMT recreationally strongly suggest that experiencers write about their experiences immediately upon "coming down."

Perhaps this is one reason why Dr. Strassman did not observe much positive carryover into the daily lives of DMT experiencers. He noted that the momentary intensity of their hallucinations failed to create lasting impressions or change in the users, and he concluded that high-dose DMT experiences were not transformative.

Contrast that to people who experience near death. They typically demonstrate profound and long-lasting change such as becoming more altruistic, less materialistic, and more loving. Author and researcher Kevin Williams notes that it takes an average of seven years for individuals to integrate the transformative effects of their NDE into daily life, and that these changes typically intensify rather than fade over the course of time.[27] This was also substantiated in Pim van Lommel's study of cardiac patients, in which he interviewed patients within five days of their resuscitation, two years later, and eight years later. He found the experiencers' memories to be consistent throughout, and the transformative changes to be long lasting.

I heard from a man named Scott, who wrote that he had a near-death experience in December 1997 as a result of an acute bacterial infection. He was in the middle of a company meeting when he suddenly became exhausted. He told a coworker who immediately offered to drive him home. He described what happened next:

We headed home almost immediately, but I remember absolutely nothing until suddenly I was being loaded into an ambulance. My next image was me sitting with a loving God up in the corner of the emergency room, looking down on my body.

I saw my wife and son at the foot of the bed and thought about how much they were still grieving and suffering after burying my brother-in-law just one month earlier. I sure didn't want to add to their burden. When they called to me, I returned to my body as suddenly as I had left.

This event changed my life completely. Fifteen years later, I still have a "fire in my bones" for the Lord! My first wife of thirty-one years divorced me because I wasn't the guy I used to be. Instead of trying to climb the corporate ladder of success,

I now feel moved to feed the homeless, work in food banks, and run a hospital, nursing home, and hospice ministry. I eat, work, play, sleep, and dream Jesus. I'm definitely not the guy I used to be—I'm better!

—SCOTT, OKLAHOMA CITY, OK

Although the myth of DMT's ability to explain the NDE phenomenon has become widespread, it is based entirely on speculation. Clearly something else is going on that science has yet to uncover.

WHEN A LIFE STORY GOES FURTHER THAN SCIENCE

The more I understood the research, the less I understood about my survival.

By the time my body was pulled from the river, my skin was purple, cold, and waxy. I had fixed and dilated pupils. I was not breathing and had no heartbeat. My companions, who are professional raft and kayak instructors as well as being EMT trained and experienced, believed me to be dead. They continue to claim they had little to do with my survival other than providing the hands through which God's will was accomplished.

I had taken my quest as far as medical science could go, but my life clearly went further. The NDE I had was definitely *not* a product of a dream or of my imagination. It was not a seizure or neurotransmitter-induced hallucination, and it was not the effect of my circumstances or of my brain naturally shutting down that current science could explain. I had experienced an outside-of-the-visible-universe, outside-of-known-natural-laws, out-of-the-body—which is to say, supernatural—event.

Chapter 6

—

CROSSING OVER AND COMING BACK

*"Life is eternal; and love is immortal;
and death is only a horizon; and a horizon is nothing
save the limit of our sight."*

—ROSSITER RAYMOND

For ancient Greek and Roman sailors, the Pillars of Hercules, at the eastern end of the Mediterranean, marked the edge of the known world. The pillars were said to bear the warning *Non plus ultra*—"nothing farther beyond." The implied message was clear: The unknown is dangerous. Turn back before it's too late.

But you're reading this book as an act of courage, and where the big questions are concerned, you're not inclined to turn back. You want to see beyond the horizon of your life now. You want to know what to expect after you or a loved one passes from this earth. Or you may want to see how a personal experience like mine lines up with what you believe to be true based on scripture.

Look at this book as a voyager's report. In my near-death experience, I traveled past the horizon of my time on Earth, and now I'm telling you what I heard, saw, felt, and came to know. But it's important for you to know that even though my report is based on personal experience, it does not stand alone.

In this chapter we look at the reports of other "travelers," from times past to the present. The fact is, countless examples of NDEs can be found in the historical records, and all the descriptions share striking similarities with those of modern-day accounts.

Our current understanding of these encounters is due largely to the work of Drs. Raymond Moody and Elizabeth Kübler-Ross, psychiatrists who were early pioneers in the study of NDEs. Through the work of Moody, Kübler-Ross, Peter Fenwick, Pim van Lommel, and many others, the clinical phenomenon of NDEs has now been well documented. Surprisingly, it has actually been found to be quite common, occurring in up to 18 percent of people who were declared "clinically dead" before resuscitation.[1]

Think about it! This equates to millions of people who steadfastly claim to have had this sort of experience. And this doesn't even consider the fact that most people who have this sort of supernatural experience never mention it to anyone.

Perhaps skepticism of NDEs reflects a fear not unlike the ancient Greek and Roman fear of what lies beyond—beyond the pillars of death. Just as we now know that undiscovered oceans and continents waited beyond the Pillars of Hercules, we also know that God holds an eternity of goodness in store for us beyond the horizon of physical death.

DEFINING THE NEAR-DEATH EXPERIENCE

The term "near-death experience" was coined by Dr. Raymond Moody in 1975[2] and describes a recognizable constellation of hyperintense and powerful perceptions, insights, and sensory experiences that occur in situations of death, near death, or other dire circumstances. What distinguishes an NDE from the common event of dying is that the person doesn't stay physically dead or unconscious—the person returns from the apparent death to full consciousness, and often to full functioning. What an NDE suggests is that the journey between life and death is not always unidirectional.

No one, least of all me, is proposing that our physical bodies won't eventually die—after all, mortality is a fundamental part of the human experience. But for reasons we struggle to understand, some people die or come very close to dying but are then given a return ticket, extending their time on Earth.

A UNIVERSAL HUMAN PHENOMENON

If the NDE phenomenon is a universal human one, you'd expect accounts of these experiences to occur in all eras, and the world over. And that is the case. Although details and terminology vary slightly by culture, accounts of NDEs have been reported throughout the world, as far back as 1760 BC, and in the traditions of Christians, Hindus, Buddhists, Muslims, Jews, and Native Americans.[3]

Plato's *Republic,* written about 420 BC, was the first account of an NDE in Western literature. In this book, Plato tells the account of Er, who died in battle but revived on his funeral pyre. Er went on to tell others of his journey into the afterlife, which included many similarities to modern-day descriptions:

> *With many other souls as his companions, Er had come across an awe-inspiring place with four openings—two into and out of the sky and two into and out of the earth. . . . Meanwhile from the other opening in the sky, clean souls floated down, recounting beautiful sights and wondrous feelings. . . . They reached a*

place where they could see a rainbow shaft of light brighter than any they had seen before. . . . . After this each soul was assigned a guardian spirit to help them through their life.[4]

Although most of us weren't taught this in Sunday school, it's reasonable to understand several accounts in the Bible where people came back to life as NDEs (e.g., 1 Kings 17:17–21, Luke 7:12–15, John 11:1–44, Acts 9:36–41, Acts 20:9–10).

In the first century after Christ, the apostle Paul wrote a classic report of an NDE. Perhaps expressing the limits of understanding and expression common to the experience, he chose to write about his experience in the third person: "I know a man in Christ who fourteen years ago was caught up to the third heaven. Whether it was in the body or out of the body I do not know—God knows. . . . [He] was caught up to paradise and heard inexpressible things" (2 Corinthians 12:2–4).

Later in the same passage he calls what he heard "surpassingly great revelations" (12:7) that he wasn't permitted to describe in full.

Further Christian writings about NDEs include those of Gregory the Great, the sixth-century pope. In *The Dialogues,* Gregory describes more than forty other NDEs. For example, he recorded the firsthand account of Stephen, a prominent businessman who died while on a trip to Constantinople. You'll see parallels between my account in the previous chapter and the account that follows:

Three years ago, as you know, this same Stephen died in the virulent plague which devastated this city [Rome], in which arrows were seen coming down from the sky and striking people dead. A certain soldier in this city of ours happened to be struck down. He was drawn out of his body and lay lifeless, but he soon returned [to life] and described what befell him. At that time there were many people experiencing these things.

He said that there was a bridge, under which ran a black, gloomy river, which breathed forth an intolerably foul-smelling vapor. But across the bridge, there were delightful meadows carpeted with green grass and sweet-smelling flowers. The meadows seemed to be meeting places for people clothed in white. Such a pleasant odor filled the air that the sweet smell by itself was enough to satisfy [the hunger of] the inhabitants who were strolling there. In that place each one had his own separate dwelling, filled with magnificent light. A house of amazing capacity was being constructed there, apparently out of golden bricks, but he could not find out for whom it might be. On the bank of the river there were dwellings, some of which were contaminated by the foul vapor that rose up from the river, but others were not touched at all.[5]

While NDEs are uniquely individual, and may only contain a few of the same components, the overall combination of components is consistent worldwide. Even young children, whose experiences are unlikely to be the result of preexisting beliefs or expectations, report descriptions identical to those of adults.

Individuals who have an NDE always know that something profound has occurred, but often don't know what to think about it or how to process it. I have personally listened to the near-death stories of hundreds of people, and I have frequently been one of the first people to be told about it. Many people keep such an experience to themselves for many years. Why? Some worry that the significance and sense of sacredness of their experience will be diminished by sharing it, some fear the experience itself, but mostly people fear the disbelief of other people. They don't want to be thought of as crazy, deceived, or "one of those religious zealots."

If a witness as theologically profound as the apostle Paul found himself at a loss for words to describe his NDE, we shouldn't be surprised that others also falter. Universally, in fact, people describe their NDEs as being beyond description and declare that even art and metaphor cannot begin to capture the true experience. As such, individual descriptions can seem incomplete or frustratingly vague. But don't let that keep you from seeing the overarching truth: There is a convincing consistency within the accounts that researchers find fascinating, and that I hope you find persuasive.

COMMON ELEMENTS OF NDES

What are these commonalities? Some of the most frequent ones mentioned include the following.

1. A Deep Sense of Well-Being Infused with Pure Love

Without a doubt the foremost component of NDEs is the universal experience of feeling wholly and unabashedly loved and accepted by the pure Source of all love, which most people identify in some way as God. I have spoken with a few people who had an NDE in which they initially experienced what they described as hell, complete with fear, anxiety, and despair. Yet each one claimed to have, ultimately, been pulled away from that reality by God's love.

This feeling of being immersed in God as total, unadulterated love is actually the most profound, memorable, and defining aspect of my entire NDE. If I ever had any doubts about the vitality of our spirits as separate entities from our flesh, the depth of love that I experienced once I was free from the confines of my body has left me utterly convinced. Trust me, words are inadequate to even begin to describe the immense reality of what I experienced, but I will do my best.

One of the first things I noticed about the purity of the love I encountered was that it displaced every other imaginable emotion. Like fear. Given the circumstances in which I found myself, fear would certainly be an appropriate response. And yet I discovered that I couldn't have mustered up a feeling of fear or anxiety even if I had tried.

I'm not sure why this was so surprising to me. After all, the apostle John seemed to understand the link between being filled by God's love and the utter displacement of fear. He wrote, "God is love. . . . There is no fear in love" (1 John 4:16, 18). I admit that reading those words in the Bible and experiencing firsthand the impact of God's love for me are two very different things.

2. Separation of Body and Spirit

Near-death experiences usually begin with a feeling of effortlessly moving through space, be it infinite darkness, infinite brilliance, through a tunnel, or along a path. This space often connects the past to the present to the future, without any real sense of time. A dimensional shift is often described and is certainly what I experienced.

People feel separated from their physical body but are often able to see their body and are aware of events going on around it. Furthermore, they are often able to accurately describe details of what was said and done while they were "dead" or relay information they could not have known beforehand. I was able to clearly see the people and their activities below me on the riverbank. I was also able to hear and understand what they were saying. Their words caused me to momentarily return to them and take a breath.

Sometimes this ability to both see and hear the events going on around them despite being unconscious or dead helps those who have had an NDE corroborate their experience to others.

Kimberly Sharp was a social worker in Harborview Medical Center when a patient named Maria was brought in after suffering a heart attack. Kim told me, and also wrote in her book *After the Light: What I Discovered on the Other Side of Life That Can Change Your World,* that Maria had been unconscious when she had been brought to the hospital. When Kimberly visited her hospital room the following day, Maria described leaving her body and floating above the hospital. Desperate to prove that she had, in fact, left her body and was not crazy, Maria told Kimberly about seeing a worn dark blue tennis shoe on the ledge outside a window on the far side of the hospital. Not believing her but wanting to help, Kimberly checked the ledge by pressing her face against the sealed windows—and found a shoe that perfectly matched the details Maria had related.[6]

My friend Robin shared with me her mother's story that occurred during knee surgery. She said that her mother suddenly found herself floating above her body. She watched as the surgeons reacted to her flatlined EKG. The surgeon, who was a longtime friend of hers, cursed when he dropped an instrument. She was eventually sent back to her body. The following day, she described the scene and everything that happened in the operating room with great accuracy and finished by saying that she had never heard her surgeon curse before—the details of which were validated by her surgeon.[7]

3. No Fear of Death

Since fear is pushed aside by God's love, it is not surprising that most people are not frightened by the separation of their body and soul, or by the experience and very recognition of their death—even if the death was sudden or traumatic.

I certainly experienced this feature. Even though I am a strong swimmer and love being in and around the water, I had always feared a drowning death. While underwater, I thought about this irony and noted that I never experienced the air hunger or panic that I had thought would be so terrifying.

Unlike the many people whose fear of death can be so paralyzing as to prevent them from fully engaging in life, few near-death experiencers harbor any lingering fear of death. Why would we? Death has no sting, so most of us have a change of perspective regarding our own death and that of others. Having experienced the reality of life after death, we view physical death as merely a transition and return to our true home.

Stephanie wrote to me that March 18, 2006, she was being monitored in the emergency room for heart issues and had been given a nitroglycerin pill when her blood pressure suddenly plummeted. She recalls:

> Then I was gone—walking along a beautiful flagstone path in a huge tree-lined field of the most brilliantly colored flowers. I felt an incredibly radiant warmth like nothing I've ever felt on Earth. Breathing was totally effortless. As I walked on that path, I had such a feeling of love, joy, and peace, which is difficult to put into words. There was absolutely no sense of time during my heavenly experience.
>
> Suddenly, I was back in the ER with about a dozen people

*crowded around me, including my very ashen husband and sob-
bing thirty-year-old daughter. I was incredibly disappointed to
be back. My daughter kept saying, "We thought we lost you."
And all I said was, "I didn't want to come back. I don't want
to be here."*

*I was not an overly religious person, although I am now very
aware of God's presence, and I love knowing that God uses me
to shine His light to others. Knowing that I may be the only
"Christ" that some people will ever see makes me really try to
see myself and others the way God sees us. I have no fear of
dying and do not mourn the passing of others as I once did. Of
course, the hard part is missing them, but I know we will be
reunited one day.*

—STEPHANIE, LOS ALTOS, CA

4. A Life Review

Most people experience some variation of a life review during their NDE. Many describe it as a fact-finding experience
rather than a fault-finding one. As details of one's life are
viewed and experienced from the perspective of each living
thing involved, the dying person usually gains new insight
and develops greater empathy and compassion. It is often one
of the NDE components that creates the most profound and
lasting change in the experiencer.

In her book *Searching for Home*, Laurelynn Martin wrote:

*By reviewing my past, I was brought to new places of discov-
ery within myself. Many events were shown simultaneously.
I recalled two examples. When I was five years old I teased
another five-year-old girl to the point of tears. I was now in a
unique position to feel what she felt. Her frustration, her tears,
and her feelings of separateness were now my feelings. I felt a*

tremendous amount of compassion for this child. I experienced how she needed love, nurturing, and forgiveness. My essence gave love to both of us—a love so deep and tender, like the love between a mother and child. I realized by hurting another, I was only hurting myself. Again, I was experiencing oneness.

The next incident was similar:

I had made fun of a scrawny, malnourished asthmatic kid. He died when he was seventeen years old from a cerebral aneurysm. He seemed to be in the realm of existence I was in. Yet, still I was not sure where I was. When this boy was twelve, he had written me a love letter that I rejected. I was experiencing his pain, which became my pain. At the same time, I felt a tremendous amount of love for this boy and myself. My contact with him went beyond the physical and I felt his soul. He had a vibrant, bright light burning inside of him. Feeling his spirit's strength and vitality was an inconceivable moment especially knowing how much he physically suffered when he was alive.[8]

5. "More Real Than Real"

People in the midst of an NDE have a heightened sense and depth of emotion, consciousness, and perceptions. Communication is always crystal clear, even when it occurs telepathically. Personally, the word *telepathic* has always sounded outlandish to me, and I hesitate to use it. But a better word to explain what happens eludes me. Even though heavenly communication does not use one's mouth, as we do on Earth, it is perfectly understood. It is almost like a blast of pure energy, blanketed in love, which is being passed from one being to another.

When describing their NDEs, people always say the same

thing I do—that the sights, sounds, sensations, and emotions are hyperintense and "more real than real." Almost everyone notes indescribable beauty. My own experience included more colors than are in a rainbow, with an intensity of color that was beyond anything I have ever experienced here on Earth. I saw them, felt them, and experienced them. Remarkably, deaf people hear and blind people see—even those who have been deaf or blind since birth. Being able to see the beauty during an NDE is all the more thought-provoking when you realize that congenitally blind people don't have visual components to their nighttime dreams or have visual hallucinations when given drugs.[9]

In their book, Ring and Cooper relate a story from a person who was born blind and had seen "no light, no shadows, nothing for forty-three years." An automobile accident and an NDE in the emergency room changed all that:

"Rising through space," he reported, "I saw lights. In the distance, I heard the most beautiful sounds, like wind chimes. They contained every single note you could imagine, from the lowest to the highest, all blended together." After a passage through a dark tunnel, he came to "a balmy, bright summer land scene of trees, where there were thousands of people singing, laughing, and talking. Flowers were everywhere in different colors and variety. Both the flowers and birds I observed in the trees seemed to have light around them. Then I saw four of my previously deceased friends. They seemed to be healed, or somehow made better."

After a loving encounter with Christ, he was told it wasn't his time yet, and he "reentered my blind world in the hospital."[10]

And there are more aspects to an NDE that many people experience.

6. Unusual Knowledge or Foresight

Like I did, at some point during their NDEs, most people experience a complete understanding of the universe and its divine order. As a result, some people return with new insights or abilities. During her NDE, Anita Moorjani visualized the cause of her cancer, which facilitated her miraculous healing after returning to Earth.[11] Tony Cicoria returned with an ability to play the piano, and Mr. Olaf Swenson says it was the advanced knowledge of quantum physics gained during his NDE that allowed him to develop more than a hundred patentable ideas in subatomic chemistry.[12] Even without retaining an understanding of complex subjects, almost everyone returns with a deep appreciation of the interconnectedness of everything and every living creature.

Occasionally near-death experiencers gain knowledge or insight into something that will happen in the future. I was told about my son's future death, as well as some other challenges that my family and I would have to face. Sometimes people are shown their future children, while others are shown other situations that influence their desire to return to Earth.

A few years ago, I spoke with a man who had been shown a troubling and dangerous future situation in which his adult children would become embroiled. He also saw how that situation could be avoided if he were present, so he reluctantly chose to return to Earth. Five years later, what he had been shown did indeed come to pass and he was able to provide the needed assistance.

7. Reunion with Friends and Relatives

While I didn't take the time to consider whether the people I encountered were known to me, none of my close relatives or friends had died before the time of my NDE. Despite that, I had a very clear sense that the people who greeted me had known and loved me for all my existence. Many other people, however, report being reunited with previously deceased relatives, friends, or guides who are brilliantly radiant and welcoming. These may be someone the experiencer knew to be dead, someone they didn't yet know to be dead, or relatives who were not previously known to the experiencer. Regardless of the previously deceased person's life circumstances or the circumstances of their death, their heavenly spirit appears as whole, healthy, joyful, and vibrant.

Occasionally, the NDE person meets someone who exposes a family secret, as it did for four-year-old Colton Burpo who met a miscarried older sibling he had never known about.[13]

When Dr. Eben Alexander had a coma-induced NDE, he desperately wanted to be greeted by his deceased father and was heartbroken when this did not occur. Instead, a sister he never knew existed, but subsequently identified, was there to guide him. Dr. Alexander has subsequently expressed gratitude for his father's absence during the NDE, as his father's presence might have caused Dr. Alexander to assume his NDE merely reflected his innermost desire, rather than being outside the realm of earthly reality.[14]

8. A Point of No Return

I've told you about the large, domed structure I approached. For me, that was the "point of no return," and I subsequently learned that an awareness of this kind of threshold is quite common. Many people approach some sort of barrier beyond which there is no return from death. At, or before reaching this barrier, the dying person is told it is not their time, or they are not ready. They then return to their body, despite rarely wanting to do so.

Steven, from New Jersey, told me this story that vividly describes his encounter with the kind of barrier I'm talking about:

When I was young, I suffered from nephritis. At age sixteen, my kidneys finally shut down, and I was rushed to the hospital after being sick at home for a few days. I was admitted to the ICU, and I felt so cold. I first heard music that was not of this earth. I was then above the hospital bed and saw my mother praying at my bedside.

I then had a thin veil-like material over my body, but I did not have a real body. I was amazed because I could put my hands through it. Next, I was in a beautiful garden, walking down a path. When I got at the end of the path, I saw a wall that I could not climb over. When I looked over, I saw a city of gold. In the middle of it was a very bright dome. Then I heard a voice call my name three times. I turned around and saw feet, a white robe, and a gold sash. He told me, "Steven, go back and live a long, happy life. But never, never forget me." In a blink, I was back. I opened my eyes and told my mother I loved her.

—STEVEN, PATTERSON, NJ

The commonalities continue even after the experience itself has ended.

9. A Certainty About Significance

Most of us who have had this sort of profound spiritual experience hold an unwavering belief that we have experienced something of immeasurable significance. Most of us feel we have learned something about the purpose of life. A majority of experiencers sense that they have entered a spiritual realm, sometimes seeing a city of lights and almost always experiencing a divine presence, an all-loving Supreme Being.

10. Perfect Playback

One feature that distinguishes NDEs and other profound spiritual encounters is that no matter how much time has passed, individuals remember the experience reliably and accurately, with unchanging details. And rather than merely recalling a memory, it is as though we are simultaneously describing what happened while reexperiencing it in the present tense.

When I was in the hospital after my kayaking accident, I described my experiences to Debbi, the wife and mother of the friends who resuscitated me. This was the era before easy electronic communication, so she wrote everything down on paper in order to tell those who were still in Chile what had happened to me after I left the country. She pulled out her long-forgotten notes before quietly listening to me one recent summer when I was being interviewed in the home of her mother-in-law. Afterward, she was wide-eyed as she excitedly exclaimed that the details of my descriptions were exactly the same as they had been when I originally described them to her almost fourteen years earlier. She was surprised with this discovery, although I wasn't.

SAME EXPERIENCE, DIFFERENT DETAILS

As I researched the near-death phenomenon, I found strong confirmation that while story details may vary, both the substance and the emotional and spiritual meaning of those stories rarely do. Skeptics often use these differences between individual details to question the validity of the NDE phenomenon, and I empathize with their cautious, even dismissive scientific standards of reproducibility. But I've come to see this response as unfortunate and misguided.

How do any of us describe or experience intense beauty? This is an almost universal component of NDE descriptions, and not surprisingly, the specific expression of that experience of beauty varies between individuals, just as it does on Earth. Think of it this way: Some of us appreciate the informational realism of photographs; others prefer the more emotive and suggestive communication of abstract paintings. For some of us, Mozart's arias move us to tears; others of us definitely prefer the gritty emotion of a country-western song.

I believe God presents to each of us at our death the experience that will speak most powerfully and directly to us, whether that is music, dance, flowers, animals, or some other deep expression of beauty. Why wouldn't our loving Creator want to welcome us home with the language of our heart?

In my view, the variation in experience speaks even more strongly to NDEs *not* being the result of mere physiology. If the NDE experience were nothing more than a chemical or physiological response, I would expect more consistency. In my medical practice, for example, I have treated scores of people who have broken a bone. Their pain response is largely dictated by physiology, and its course is quite predictable. Such is not the case with NDEs.

PROFOUND CHANGE OF PERSPECTIVE

One feature of NDEs is remarkably consistent, though, and clearly points to a higher dimension of reality. As I've mentioned, most experiencers lose all fear of death but gain a universal belief in life after death. Even those who died as atheists don't just *think* there is a God—they *know* there is.

Lifestyles and core beliefs change. Materialists become altruists, alcoholics are often unable to imbibe, and strict religious dogma tends to give way to grace. Most of us come back determined to make a difference in the world, and with a heightened awareness of and appreciation for the present moment.

After my own return, my husband remarked that I didn't seem to care about anything anymore. But it wasn't that I didn't care, just that what I cared about had dramatically shifted and deepened. He didn't realize that, although I now felt entirely removed from the cares and values of this world, I cared very deeply about what I believed was of eternal importance.

And this is true for many others. Most people become significantly more spiritual after an NDE, regardless of their religious background, and many return with increased psychic or intuitive abilities. Sometimes NDEs even create lasting objective physical changes such as lower blood pressure, or measurably altered electrical fields.[15]

KNOWING THE UNKNOWN IS . . . COMPLICATED

But for most people, the return to Earth and to a physical life is also a complex and confusing event. While people who have had an NDE rejoice in their encounter with unconditional love and acceptance, experiencers often feel a sense of isolation and confusion upon return to their previous life. While there is sometimes guilt at not wanting to come back, there is also depression at having returned. Many struggle with understanding their experience and how to incorporate it into their life. Recognizing the immortality of their soul, most experiencers have a greater sense of purpose for their earthly journey, and many become more driven and determined to make a difference in the world, but some are unsure about how to do so. These emotional and behavioral changes are not always accepted or understood by loved ones, often leading to strained or severed friendships and marriages.

As for me, after many months of research, discussion, and consideration, I concluded that my experience had been real and true. In accepting this conclusion, however, I was also accepting the reality of all that I had been told regarding my work on Earth and my future challenges. While it was electrifying to have had this experience, it was also a heavy burden. I was scared and felt isolated and lonely. No one, including the people closest to me, could possibly understand what I had experienced. I couldn't admit to them that I hadn't wanted to return, something impossible to understand outside the context of God's love, and I couldn't tell them about the challenges we were about to face.

Yet, about one thing I was absolutely certain—heaven is real, and I had been there.

Chapter 7

A GUIDED TOUR OF HEAVEN

"Joy is the serious business of heaven."

—C. S. Lewis

As I speak across the country about my experiences, a crowd invariably lines up afterward to talk. Trust me, it's not because I'm an unusually riveting speaker. What compels them to linger, often for several hours, are their own stories and questions. Some want to know if they'll see their departed loved ones again, or if their departed loved ones know what is happening now on Earth. Some are wrestling with their own mortality, or the recent death of someone they cherished. Some just want to personally look into my eyes and ask me if it's all true. But what people ask about more than anything else is heaven. Everyone wants to know what lies beyond the veil.

I often say that my story, and the truths it reveals about who God is and what he wants for us, is for everybody. But I also acknowledge that mine is a Christian experience. The Jesus who comforted me while I was drowning, and spoke with me in that beautiful field, was the Lord I knew from prior experience and from scripture. What a person of another faith or no faith experiences in an NDE, I simply cannot say. For example, I have no idea if there are different heavens or different parts of heaven. Some version of heaven is described in the texts of all major religions and, like my own descriptions, is consistently noted to be extraordinarily beautiful, gardenlike, and the place of our eternal home.

What I know for certain is that I was somewhere other than in my body, it was glorious, and Jesus was there with me. This is my testimony.

Most of us are familiar with biblical descriptions of heaven, but even those come with limitations. In the book of Revelations, we read that heaven "shone with the glory of God, and its brilliance was like that of a very precious jewel, like a jasper, clear as crystal" (Revelation 21:11). Notice how important the word *like* is in almost every description of heaven. That's because the closest we can come to an accurate description is to compare the qualities of heaven with something we understand from Earth. The word *paradise* might come close to capturing the essence of heaven in our language, but even that is limited.

When people ask me to get as specific as possible with what I learned, here are the questions I hear most, and what I say in response.

"WILL WE KNOW EACH OTHER IN HEAVEN? WILL WE SEE OUR LOVED ONES?"

My experience, the experience of many others, and the biblical texts deliver a definite yes to these questions. We will definitely know each other in heaven and we will absolutely see our loved ones. Almost immediately after leaving my body, I was greeted by a group of beings who were simultaneously familiar and unfamiliar. This may sound strange and perhaps even unsettling, but I can assure you that I felt nothing but peace and happiness in their fellowship. I received a very warm welcome into heaven and immediately felt right at home.

Grace, whose testimony appears in Cherie Sutherland's book *Within the Light*,[1] describes an experience similar to mine:

> *There seemed to be figures, grouped, almost a theatrical grouping, like a stage set. And at first they were just amorphous, shadowy figures and I was peripherally but intensely aware of a grouping on my right, ahead of me, but I hadn't really looked at it. I knew it was there but it was not impinging on my consciousness too much at that stage—I was too busy looking the other way. And as I looked, one of the figures seemed to resolve itself, and I thought, "I know that face," and I suddenly realized, "Oh God, it's my aunty Hannah," who died eleven years ago. And then I saw my uncle Abraham, who died before I was born. . . . I knew they were there to see me, and they knew me, even though they'd never met me.*

Could I have identified the individuals who welcomed me? If I had been there longer, or paid greater attention when I was there, I believe I could have done so. I liken it to one's attending a large gathering of relatives but not quite being able to remember each person's name, to whom they are married, or how they are connected to you, but knowing they are family. Regardless, I was delighted by their presence and immediately knew they were people who were part of my "life circle" or "soul group," for lack of better terms, with whom I have an eternal bond.

THE FOURTH LESSON THAT HEAVEN REVEALS

Heaven is a reality where we are made whole—no
pain, no sorrow, no suffering—understanding prevails,
relationships are reconciled, and we will be with God
and our loved ones forever.

I have experienced the deep pain of losing people I dearly love, and it is a great comfort to me to know that when I next return to heaven, my son and all the other people I love who have gone before me will be there waiting. I look forward to this time with great anticipation.

"WHAT DO PEOPLE IN HEAVEN LOOK LIKE?"

Those who greeted me on the pathway appeared to have a normal physical form, yet they also seemed ageless, appearing neither old nor young, fat nor skinny, dark nor light. Each of the beings I met was beautifully radiant and exquisitely vibrant. In fact, it was their luminosity that made their forms and faces somewhat indistinct, and it reminded me of why angels and saints are often drawn with halos.

Their brilliance should have been blinding, but it wasn't. Casting no shadows, it seemed to be generated from within, rather than from an external source. I, too, seemed to absorb and radiate this brilliance. They were wearing robes that appeared to be woven of fabric made from millions of shimmering filaments, actively radiating both color and love. Describing the robes and physical attributes of these spirits is like trying to describe the ethereal and constantly changing spectacle of the aurora borealis, or northern lights. They appeared somewhat solid, and I was unable to see through them, yet they simultaneously appeared pearlescent and translucent.

Is this how people in heaven always appear? Did they take on human form so that I would recognize them, know their love, and not be afraid? I really don't know, but it's fun to wonder.

"DID YOU HAVE A BODY IN HEAVEN?"

I wore a robe similar to the ones that the other spirits were wearing. It flowed as I moved, but I had no sense of its fabric moving against my skin. I had no sense of its weight or mass. Actually, I don't really know if I even had skin. Like the others, I seemed to also have a physical form, but there were no mirrors and, truthfully, I never thought to look. Although now I wish I had taken more mental notes, it just didn't seem important at the time, especially since I had no plans to return to Earth or share my story if I did return.

I will say that I still seemed very much like "me," but with all my flaws and limitations removed. I was still aware of my earthly life and journey, but I think I was experiencing the perfect "me" that God sees.

We were standing, sometimes jubilantly dancing about, and occasionally sitting, but there was no sense of weightlessness or of gravity. We just sort of existed in the space. Although we joyfully embraced, I have no conscious memory of the brush of their garments, or what they felt like beneath my fingertips. I don't remember a feeling of breathing or swallowing and never thought of a need for nourishment. I clearly smelled the intense fragrance of the flowers that surrounded me, but I have no recollection of other smells.

Although my husband is very musical and will likely hear

symphonies in heaven, I did not. I have no ability to sing, don't know sharps from flats, and can't hear the nuances of sophisticated music, so angels performing a symphony while sitting on the clouds might not have inspired me to stay long. I was able to hear what sounded like the rustling of a gentle breeze, and I heard a musical harmonic of some sort when I was on the arched threshold. It was as though the joy emanating from all the souls and angels I saw was merging to create a perfectly harmonious song of praise. When I looked back down at the scene on the riverbank, I could also hear the normal voices of my boating companions as they were performing CPR. But while I could also "hear" and understand the voices of my spiritual companions, I did not hear them as distinct sounds. I would not, for example, be able to describe them as high or low, male or female.

All my senses seemed to be expanded. I did not merely hear the sounds that reached my ears or detect the smells that reached my nose. I felt like I could "hear" color and "smell" sunshine.

"WAS ANYONE SICK OR HURT IN HEAVEN?"

No. This restoration to health and wholeness is described by all who have had an NDE or dream visitation. Loved ones who died in illness are restored to health, and those who were crippled in life are restored to strength. I can't begin to tell you how important this fact is for me personally. My son's body was mangled after he was struck by the car of a young man who was distractedly driving, but when I subsequently saw him during a dream visitation, which I will describe in a later chapter, he was whole, strong, and vibrant.

Then there's Geoff, who shared with me the details of his NDE. He first told of the traumatic birth that led to his cerebral palsy. His legs never worked well, and he struggled to walk. Several years prior to speaking with me, he was involved in a car accident in which he suffered grave injuries and almost died. His heart stopped several times, during which he described leaving his body and going to heaven. He said that he suddenly looked around and saw that he was in a golden field. He saw his beloved grandmother at the other end and was shocked to discover that his legs worked perfectly when he began running to her. He was equally surprised to see his grandfather waving to him, looking nothing like the elderly, cancer-ridden person he had been at the time of his death several months earlier.

People who were mean and bitter on Earth are loving and joyful in heaven. This may not be welcome news to those who have told me about relatives and friends who hurt them that they never want to forgive or see again. I found understanding in heaven. Relationships that were contentious or broken on Earth are restored to love in heaven.

"DO YOU THINK LOVED ONES IN HEAVEN CAN SEE US HERE ON EARTH?"

I believe the answer is yes. My experience of being simultaneously aware of what was happening in heaven and also what was going on behind me on Earth opened my eyes to the possibility that spirits really do cross into our world.

In addition, after listening to hundreds share with me their own stories of NDEs and spiritual encounters, I've concluded that the spirits of our deceased loved ones are not completely removed from our earthly existence. (Not that I can entirely explain this, of course.) I believe they are aware of us, and our life events, that they are our greatest cheerleaders, and I believe they are able to sporadically cross into our world. I've just heard too many stories of this occurrence to ignore the possibility.

While I was in heaven, I did not forget my earthly life. I was able to see and understand everything that was happening on the riverbank. I thought about my husband and my children, my parents, and siblings. I've never been able to figure out how to describe this, but as I thought of each one, I was able to empathetically be a part of them, transferring a feeling that everything is "fine." It was as if a part of my spirit traveled to wherever they were at that moment and interjected an emotional sense of contentment into their psyche. I did feel some disappointment at not returning to them and sharing their life journey, but I was confident they would be fine. I was equally confident that I would continue to love them, still be a part of their lives, and be reunited with them when their own work on Earth was done. It is interesting, though not surprising, to note that I thought and remembered a great deal about my relationships while I was in heaven, but not at all about my work or other earthly issues that occupy so much of our time and attention.

Although I don't know what prompts the ability to cross into our physical world, I don't believe that our loved ones cross over at our request. I wonder, though, if sometimes God allows them to come to us in order to bring comfort and assurance.

"ARE THERE ANIMALS IN HEAVEN?"

I have been asked many times if I encountered animals during my time in heaven, but I did not. Animals, however, are one of God's wonderful creations here on Earth, so it would make sense that they would also be in God's heavenly world.

In fact, the words of Isaiah 65:25 imply there are animals

in heaven, and many people have recounted seeing animals during their NDEs. P. M. H. Atwater has observed that, "animals are often seen during near-death episodes, either as part of the scenario or as that initial greeter or guide."[2]

Bryce Bond[3] had an NDE after being rushed to the hospital after a violent allergic reaction. He remembered passing through a long tunnel toward a brilliant light. He describes what happened next:

> I put my dog on the ground and stepped forward to embrace my stepfather when a very strong voice is heard in my consciousness. Not yet, it says. I scream out, "Why?" Then this inner voice says, "What have you learned, and whom have you helped?" I am dumbfounded. The voice seems to be from without as well as within. Everything stops for a moment. I have to think of what was asked of me. I cannot answer what I have learned, but I can answer whom I have helped.
>
> I feel the presence of my dog around me as I ponder those two questions. Then I hear barking, and other dogs appear, dogs I once had. As I stand there for what seems to be an eternity, I want to embrace and be absorbed and merge. I want to stay.

About her NDE after a heart attack, as described in her book *The Other Side of Death*, Jan Price writes:

> I suppose we never really think of ourselves as dying, but obviously I had died because I wasn't in my body anymore. . . . Suspended in the ocean of blue, golden streams of light—like stardust—began to pour through me. . . . As the density changed, becoming lighter and finer, I felt that I was being lifted to another level of awareness—and then I found myself

*in surroundings that appeared to be more substantial. Maggi
was there. My beautiful dog, my beloved Springer, came to me.
She had died less than a month before, and John and I still
ached from her absence. I felt her presence, her love, and she appeared to me as she had when she was in physical form—only
younger, more vital.*[4]

I believe that at our time of death, God presents to each of
us the experience that we not only will understand, but will
also make us feel loved and unafraid. I agree completely with
evangelist Billy Graham who said, "God will prepare everything for our perfect happiness in heaven, and if it takes my
dog being there, I believe he'll be there."

"IS THERE A HELL?"

Hell was not part of my experience, but other people have
described their terrifying and hellish experiences near death.
In each case, though, they have said they were ultimately
saved by God's love.

While I don't personally have an answer to this question
of hell, I firmly believe that God not only continually, and
eternally, offers His love, but that He always gives us the freedom to reject it. Some people have argued that no one in
their right mind who died and discovered that God (and hell)
is actually real would then reject God's love. But I have seen
that it happens. Inexplicably, the hearts of some people become so hardened, and their eyes so blinded, that they steadfastly reject God's truth, even as He is made known to them
in their transition from death.

"IS THERE SADNESS IN HEAVEN?"

Absolutely none—no tears or pain, no anxiety or worry, no anger or hatred, and people are restored to health and wholeness. Heaven is a place where God lives and is worshipped (Revelation 4:8–11, Deuteronomy 26:15) and is a place of exceeding joy (Matthew 13:44). Yes, everyone there will know Jesus to be his son, and the one who bridges the gap and makes it possible for us to be there, but it is still God's house. His love for us is so overpowering, so visceral, and so real that sadness, pain, and mourning don't stand a chance.

The verse that comes to my mind is a stunning promise of things to come for those who want to be in heaven with God. "He will wipe away every tear from their eyes. There will be no more death or mourning or crying or pain, for the old order of things has passed away" (Revelation 21:4).

"WHAT WAS YOUR BIGGEST SURPRISE?"

I was stunned by my lack of fear and lack of desire to return to Earth. I was most astonished, however, by the discovery that God's promises are actually, amazingly, and abundantly true. I had *hoped* they were true and *believed* that they were, but both hope and faith contain elements of doubt. I was often unsure that spirituality and science could comfortably coexist. So I was surprised to find that spirituality and science are never actually in conflict.

Still, you might be wondering, *But so what? What difference does heaven make for me right now?*

The most important point—and one I urge you to consider as well—is that these glimpses into heaven are meant to change how you and I live now. When just before his death, Jesus told his followers that "in my Father's house are many rooms," he wasn't simply satisfying their idle curiosity; he was giving them a glimpse of heaven for a practical earthly reason. He knew they were frightened and needed comfort. And he understood, I believe, that the truths of heaven and the Father's love would empower them on their great mission of sharing the good news.

That's why I say that my journey to the gates of heaven is not actually "my" story, but only mine to share. And in a very real way, the same is true for you. You know now that death is not the end, that love will win, and that your heavenly Father has prepared an eternity of blessing for those who want to receive it. There is a heaven, and there is life after death—and that truth is meant to change how we live now for the better. Telling His story, and living it every day, is our most important task.

Chapter 8

MIRACLES ARE ALWAYS IN THE MAKING

"The most astonishing thing about miracles is that they happen."

—G. K. CHESTERTON

I remember a tall, distinguished-looking man in Southern California who waited to speak with me after I had shared my story. I'll call him George. As we chatted, George told me he was a successful businessman, a lifelong Christian, and very active in his church. Then he leaned in conspiratorially, as if to protect us from being overheard, and asked, "What *really* happened?"

I've heard that question many times, and—this might surprise you—most often from people of faith.

You might find it a bit strange, as I do, that people like George readily accept biblical stories of God's miracles yet so often hesitate to believe accounts of miracles *today*. Our belief system is based on a belief in the supernatural, but too many of us are ready to limit that reality in our own lives. Trouble is, we reject God's transformative power in the process. We claim "all things are possible with God," but we mostly mean that in theory, not in the practical every day.

Why? It's not like God changed the moment you and I

showed up on the planet! God's ability to act in his world remains the same yesterday, today, and tomorrow. When he speaks of himself in scripture, it's nearly always in the present tense—not "I was," or "I'm going to be," but "I am." I love to meditate on the beautiful promise of Jesus. "Surely I am with you always, to the very end of the age" (Matthew 28:20).

In this chapter I want to explore the reality of miracles in our lives. A miracle is when the seemingly impossible happens. But we can flesh that definition out a bit to say that a miracle is an event that the forces of nature—including humans—cannot produce on their own and that can only be explained as an act of God. Also, we usually think of a miracle as being amazing and desirable. And since God is the source, it only makes sense that a miracle advances His divine purposes in the world, while evoking our awe and gratitude.

An important purpose of this chapter is to show you that all of us can speak from personal experience about miracles, because miracles large and small are woven through all of our lives. I'll share more of my own experiences here and report some of the inspiring miracle stories others have shared with me. We'll look also at closely related phenomena: coincidences (which can be part of miracles but are not the same thing), so-called "nudges," and divine appointments.

At least a hundred and twenty-five miracles are recorded in scripture. Some, like the rainbow God sent after the Flood as a reminder of the covenant between Him and the people, were quite dramatic (Genesis 9:13). Others were more subtle.

Miracles matter—a lot! And I don't just mean for those who have dramatic personal stories to tell. If we truly let the reality of miracles into our minds and hearts, we change. We can begin to live in a way that more deeply reflects the greatness and goodness of our God. We can leave behind doubts and confusion and move into the freedom of living with absolute trust. I came back from heaven realizing that my loving God wants me to go through every day in the settled assurance that a power greater than my failures—greater even than matter, time, and circumstance—is at work in my life, in your life, and in our world *today*.

FOR THOSE WHO HAVE EYES TO SEE

I believe that miracles occur in every person's life. Seeing them, though, most often requires paying attention to details, recognizing synchronicity, acknowledging implausible odds, and giving credit to God. In *To Heaven and Back,* I mentioned that flowers deeply move my soul and "speak" to me, and I told the stories of the Bradford pear blossoms at my mother's home and of the alpine roses at my own home. The circumstances surrounding the sudden appearance of blossoms on my mother's Bradford pear tree immediately after the death of my stepfather made me wonder if they could have been a gift from my stepfather and from our supernatural God—a miracle to show God's continued presence during a time of sorrow, and a way of letting us know that everything was okay and my stepfather was happily in heaven.

When blossoming bushes of the same type and shade of the alpine rose blossoms that filled the field in which my son died inexplicably appeared in my front yard after my son's death, my skepticism that God would choose to use flowers as a means of communication was pushed aside by gratitude. My son had known the story of the Bradford pear blossoms and had known how meaningful and comforting their appearance had been to me. I believe the choice of these particular blossoms and their sudden appearance were a message from God's world to ours.

In the years since my oldest son's death, I have found a single alpine rose growing in every location that is, or has become, important to me. This occurs so predictably that I am no longer even surprised when I find them. I simply accept their message of love, comfort, and confirmation, and am filled with awe for a God who knows the language of my life. Many other people have reported similar experiences to me. They have told me that after the death of a loved one, they have been followed by butterflies, or repeatedly found coins, feathers, ladybugs, or something else that was significant to the deceased person. These are not dramatic miracles, of course, but I do believe they are divinely sent to bring hope and remind us of His presence.

A woman named Darla, from Wisconsin, told me of a similar experience: "After our grandson died, we had close visitations from a beautiful bright red cardinal. This bird visits regularly, going to one of three windows almost daily. I feel like God is giving me peace, letting me know my grandson is with Him and is okay. Since this has happened, so many people have told me of similar visits of birds. I believe God uses His creation to comfort us."

Stella wrote to tell me about seeing God in a flock of birds. As she so poignantly says, "God reaches out in the smallest ways":

My mom loved birds and she made sure she fed them every day, filling the bird feeders. When she passed away, I wanted to continue feeding the birds for her, but time had passed and I kept forgetting. One day I was sitting outside in the yard and saw that there were no more birds coming to the feeder because of my negligence. I started to cry, thinking of how much I missed my mom. Then I prayed and asked God to forgive me for not keeping up with the feeders.

All of a sudden I felt such loving presence come over me, and I looked up and I saw so many birds flying over me. They flew from one tree to another and then to the bird feeders. I hadn't seen any birds in the yard for several weeks. I knew then that God was speaking to me and telling me that everything was going to be all right, and He would help me through my grief of losing my mom. God reaches out in the smallest ways, and if we don't listen, we might miss His miracles. As is written in the Psalms, "Be still and know that I am God" (Psalm 46:10).

—STELLA, ASHEVILLE, NC

COINCIDENCE OR MIRACLE IN THE MAKING?

Signs and miracles often seem to fall outside the boundaries of natural laws, but increasingly I believe they only fall outside of our ability to understand. When a person lifts a weight off the ground, the natural law of gravity is not actually violated. Gravitational force is not absent when the weight is lifted, but a stronger force has overcome it. Miracles occur when God's desire and power overcome lesser forces.

Coincidences are often compared to miracles, but they are different. Coincidence typically describes two unplanned events that occur at the same time, while miracles represent statistically improbable constellations of events or outcomes. The more improbable the synchronous events, the more likely they are to represent a miracle.

It would be a fortunate coincidence if a man in desperate need of $836.23 walked down a street and found an envelope containing $900. It would likely be a miracle if, instead, the man found an envelope containing $836.23. But it would be a clear miracle if that same man found the envelope with $836.23 only because he was walking on that street in order to see a long-lost girlfriend whose address he was given by a taxi driver whom the man only met because his previously dependable alarm clock did not signal him to wake up that morning, causing him to miss his transportation to work, resulting in his taking a taxi, in which he discovered the driver, who had never driven this route and was substituting for a friend who was ill, was from the same hometown and had just moved to an apartment . . . next door to the man's long-lost girlfriend!

I'm having fun, but I'm sure you get the point.

While it is true that a single improbable event is likely to be commonplace and may, therefore, represent chance, it's quite reasonable to believe that multiple improbable events occurring at just the right time, in just the right sequence, are anything less than the result of God's direct intervention, the work of His angels, or the work of the Holy Spirit.

Marie sent me a story of how an apparent coincidence was clearly more than that, given her determination to end her life:

I believe that nudges and quick decisions to change our minds can come from the Holy Spirit and of angels, not luck or coincidence. When I was seventeen, I was in a very difficult place. I had just been moved into a foster home after disclosing that my father had been molesting me for several years. So damaged and lost, I would use running as my escape. My foster home sat right on the edge of the Puget Sound, so I would go there to run along the train track or the beach.

One particular day, I felt I could no longer stay on this earth. Too much pain and loneliness. So I decided I would run on a part of the track that had a blind curve ahead and just stay on it, hoping a train would come and hit me. It was stormy out that day—clouds, rain, and wind. Waves crashing on the rocks threw water onto the tracks. I wanted to feel the waves hit

*my hand, just for a second. I stepped off that train track and
kneeled down to touch the salty water.*

*Just as I leaned over to feel the water, a cargo train came bar-
reling around the corner and sped past so close to me I had to
hold on to the rocky cliff next to me to keep my balance.*

*I knew at that moment that I was meant to step off those
tracks at that precise time or I would have been hit by the train.
I felt that God and his angels were truly adjusting my path to
reflect his plan for me. I felt such love at that moment, knowing
that I was important and could not leave the earth yet.*

—MARIE, SEATTLE, WA

I agree that some religious people go overboard in calling
almost every unlikely event a miracle. On the other hand, to
think that every miracle is nothing more than coincidence
is equally careless. Some of my favorite "personal miracle"
stories come in the context of how we meet our life partners.
Maybe you have one of your own. The following story of
how Bill found Hillary has (almost) nothing to do with a
former president and first lady:

*"Too many coincidences for it to be random," says Bill, who
has been married to Hillary for sixteen years.*

*Bill and Hillary met because Bill's mother and Hillary's
father were high school friends, who hadn't been in touch for
years, when they reconnected by chance.*

*When they realized in conversation that one had a son
named Bill, one had a daughter named Hillary, and that the
Clintons were in the White House at the time, they thought
it was terribly funny. When they discovered that both children
lived in New York City, Bill's mother gave her son Hillary's
phone number and insisted that he had to call.*

Although he discovered that he and Hillary, in a city of more than seven million people, actually lived in the same neighborhood, on the same street, and in the same building, he decided not to call . . . until he ran into a former coworker in the lobby of his building.

"I said to her, 'What are you doing in my lobby?'" recalled Bill. "She said, 'Ah, I have a really good friend that lives in your building.' And I said, 'Who is that?' And she said, 'Hillary K . . .' I said, 'Oh my god. I have her number in my pocket!'" [1]

AWARE OF NUDGES AND WHISPERS

Once we realize how easily our awareness of miracles can get lost in the clatter and busyness of our lives, you and I can begin the wonderful adventure of waking up to the supernatural all around us.

But where does waking up to miracles start? We'll get as practical as possible on this question in Part Two, but here I want to talk about nudges. What many call a nudge is a gentle prompt by the Holy Spirit or an angel to pay attention to something, or do something, that we might not have otherwise done. Unlike impulses that come from our own desires or needs, the kind of prompt I'm talking about here is always related to God's will and work. A nudge is quiet, easy to overlook or ignore, and often internal. But the stories of what happens when we take the risk to respond are everywhere, once you start listening and looking. Consider the story a nudge that Bart wrote to tell me about:

At age twenty-two, I was body surfing at Huntington Beach, California, and I didn't realize the undertow was pulling me out to sea. I probably was out more than a mile in heavy surf.

The riptide was too strong to swim to shore, so I went underwater four times. While at the bottom, touching the sand with my feet, I prayed, "God, please save me. I don't want to die at the bottom of the ocean."

As soon as I finished the prayer, I found myself at the surface, but I didn't make one stroke to get there. Then a young man swam over to me to try to save me. We were both exhausted, so we alternated holding each other up until we got back to the beach. I thanked him a lot and said, "I'm sure glad you were at the beach to help save me!"

He said, "Well, I wasn't going to come to the beach today. I was tired of the beach. But as soon as I decided not to go to the beach, a voice spoke into my mind and said, 'You have to go to the beach today. You have to go.' So I did."

I believe God saved me that day and answered my prayer from twenty-five feet underwater.

—BART, HUNTINGTON BEACH, CA

Have you experienced nudges? Most people have, whether we're conscious of them or not. I responded to many nudges in the writing of my first book, but one in particular stands out.

After a week of kayaking in Arizona on the Colorado River with my family, they continued on, but I hiked out. My plan was to slowly drive back to Wyoming, visiting friends along the way. On the second day of driving, I suddenly felt a strong internal urging to return home as quickly as possible. I responded by continuing to drive rather than stopping for the night and arrived home a full day earlier than anticipated.

Early the next morning, the phone rang. I was exhausted from the trip and since no one expected me to be home, it would have been easy for me to ignore the phone. But again, an intense prompting broke through my sleepiness, and I answered. It was an agent who, uncharacteristically, had gone to her office early that morning and felt a nudge to violate her personal rule of never looking at e-mails before 11:00 a.m. She was calling me, she said, because she had received a "junk" e-mail from a television show asking if she knew anyone who had experienced near death. The inquiry required a response by that very morning. So even though she knew I was scheduled to be out of town, she decided to phone.

Do you see what happened? Both she and I had responded to nudges that were sent our way. I did appear on that television show. It was an appearance that led to a long series of opportunities to share my story about God's love and the truth of His promises.

I know what it's like to *not* respond to a nudge as well. Several months ago, I lost an opportunity to be of service to a friend, share God's love with her, and be part of the miracle of her life. A high school friend named Jenni had greatly impacted the course of my life. She was reliable, God focused, clean living, and compassionate and touched many with her quick smile and generous spirit. Her impact on my life was seemingly out of proportion to what our friendship had been, and I recently felt nudged to tell her just how important she had been to my spiritual growth. I had not spoken to her in more than twenty years and had no idea where she might be living, but I halfheartedly tried to track her down.

In reality, I didn't really want to acknowledge the internal nudge or listen to the whispers in my head. I felt awkward and silly telling a grown woman I no longer knew how significant she had been in my life's journey. I kept putting it off until the nudging became impossible to ignore. I eventually found her on a social media site and crafted a long letter to her. When I finally logged on to the site to send her my message, I was stunned to discover that she was currently on a ventilator in an intensive care unit. She died the following day without knowing of the blessing she had been to me.

Orchestrated events, many times brushed off as mere coincidence, are often used to bring about a change in direction or a miracle, but sometimes they just seem to be God's way of showing His presence in our lives. They often encourage us and help us to develop trust. Wouldn't you feel more confident in God's thoughts toward you if the following two experiences had happened to you?

About ten years ago, I was in the depths of terrible depression following a devastating divorce. I was an agnostic at that time, though beginning to question that belief. I was driving on the highway, in total despair, and I said out loud, "God, if you're real, if you actually exist, show me a sign, a really obvious sign, and then maybe I'll believe."

At that precise moment, I felt a loving presence was with me, and I saw a stand of trees in a field with a gap, revealing a billboard. On this large billboard, the single word "Jesus" appeared. Stunned, I then said, "Are you really here?" And then a semitruck changed lanes and was directly in front of me. On the back of the truck was the phrase, "Right on time."

—JUSTIN, AMARILLO, TX

When I was thirty-three years old, my life was spiraling out of control. I hated everything about my life and everyone in it. I was just not content with my life, and I was ready for something to change the path I was going down. After taking the babysitter home, I went to a local park and sat on a park bench in the dark. I cried my eyes out and turned to the Lord in prayer and asked Him to change my life or end it. I was at my wit's end.

*A "thought" came to me to go to our church, right then. I
knew that they never kept the doors opened to the church, but
I felt compelled to go anyway. I was amazed that the church
doors opened when I pulled on them. I walked down to the
altar, knelt, and begin to pray to God for forgiveness, peace,
and to take my terrible burden of worry, depression, and despair. This part of my story is a little foggy because I don't
know if it was a physical manifestation or in my spirit, but I
saw a bright light and felt a very warm feeling in my body. I
don't know if my eyes were open or not. I just know that I was
blinded by its brightness and warmth. It was incredible. I have
never felt anything like it before or since. It instantly gave me
peace that passes all understanding.*

—DAVID, LOS ANGELES, CA

Of course not everything we take as a nudge or an orchestrated event is from God. But if a thought does not recede,
my advice is to pay attention. More often than not, nudges—
especially repeated ones—are spiritual invitations to be part
of a miracle waiting to happen.

THERE WILL ALWAYS BE SKEPTICS

As I mentioned at the outset of the chapter, our first reaction
to the miraculous—even if we are people of deep faith—is
nearly always doubt. Take the preceding story from David.
Most of us immediately start to pick it apart. We wonder,
could anyone else corroborate the events? For that matter, is
David telling the truth? It seems that we almost reflexively
search for overlooked details that could explain everything.

Actually, David himself did exactly that. He assumed the
church doors had been inadvertently left unlocked, so he
called the church the following day to ask. He was assured

that security guards lock and check the doors each night and had done so last night as well. That's when David concluded that human-placed locks cannot hinder God's desires. For him, the experience opened up his belief system to the reality of a near, personally loving, and powerful God.

Consider one of the most famous miracles stories of all time—the birth of Jesus. Ignoring how Mary's pregnancy fulfilled long-standing prophecy, some skeptics claim that the virgin birth was just a lie devised by Mary and her cousin to cover up a sexual relationship with her boyfriend, Joseph. When we don't want to believe what a person has said or experienced, we cast aspersions on that individual's credibility and motives, looking for any explanation other than the possibility of a supernatural event.

Perhaps you read the story of nine-year-old Annabel Beam or saw the movie *Miracles from Heaven* about her experience. Annabel suffered from two rare, painful, and life-threatening intestinal diseases until she accidentally fell thirty feet into a hollowed-out cottonwood tree. She hit her head and had an NDE before being rescued five hours later. When she asked Jesus if she could stay with him, she was told there were plans for her that could not be fulfilled in heaven, but that there would be nothing wrong when she was sent back. Indeed, she no longer has pain, has not been hospitalized, and takes no medications. By all accounts, she has been cured of her diseases.[2]

Rather than accepting Annabel's account, people have tried to discredit her by suggesting that she suffered a concussion and had a hallucination, probably suffered from Munchausen's disease (a psychological disorder in which people fake symptoms of a disease to undergo medical treatment), and, of course, is only interested in making money from publicizing her lies.

This response seems excessive, but it is really no different from skeptics in Bible times. When Jesus restored sight to a man who had been blind from birth, people first claimed the newly sighted man was not the same man. Then they assumed he had never really been blind at all. When they could find no alternative explanation for his newly restored sight, they rejected him by hurling insults. But none of their objections were really about the man or his vision. In rejecting him, they were desperately trying to protect themselves from the possibility that miracles in the here and now could actually happen, or that Jesus might actually be God in the flesh. (You can read about it in John 9.)

It's worth asking ourselves the same question. Could our own reluctance to believe the reality of present-time miracles actually be a reflection of our own self-protectiveness? Because truly believing that miracles still happen could definitely upset our status quo, right? After all, if we accept that God is undeniably present, loving, and actively working his wonders around us, it might compel many of us to live quite differently than we are doing right now.

DIVINE APPOINTMENTS

Finally, in the category of "small miracles" are what some have called divine appointments—what feels then or later like a meeting or conversation that's been arranged in heaven. I always look for these God-arranged encounters in the midst of delays, slow traffic, or missed flights, and I often experience something beautiful.

A couple of years ago, I was on a tight schedule when I arrived with a translator for an interview at a Mexican television station. The appointed time came and passed. As more time passed, the translator became more and more agitated, as she thought about being late to our next appointment. Although she wanted to leave, I sensed that we were meant to stay, so we continued to wait.

A man who was not associated with the television station eventually walked into the lobby. Despite my natural inclination not to chat with strangers, I just knew I was meant to speak with him. Within minutes, he was in tears as he shared the sadness in his life. His mother had recently died, his wife was gravely ill in the hospital, and he felt alone. He had stopped going to church, as he was unable to see God in his sadness. In sharing some of my experiences with him, I was able not only to offer him the comfort and assurance of knowing he would see his mother again, but also to help him see the beauty that was already coming of the situation—the events in his life had prompted a reconciliation with his estranged father and initiated a beautifully developing relationship between his father and his children.

The very moment my conversation with this man concluded, a producer arrived to announce that the television station was ready for me. Until I return to heaven, I will not know the long-term impact of my conversation with this man. But I believe this was a divine appointment and that my forty-minute delay provided the moment for a small miracle to occur.

THE FIFTH LESSON THAT HEAVEN REVEALS

Big miracles happen sometimes; personal miracles happen often. God invites us to notice His miraculous presence all around.

TO HAVE OUR SIGHT RESTORED

I'm confident that stories like these—perhaps less dramatic, but no less real—are present in your past, or among your friends and family. They may include spiritual nudges, orchestrated events and divine appointments, or miracles of any shape or size. Regardless of whether these God-arranged events are dramatic, subtle, inconvenient, recognizable, or unnoticed, they occur all the time. True, many of us have been trained by cultural and religious assumptions to miss them entirely. Perhaps, like the blind man in John's gospel, we need our sight restored. We'll look more deeply in Part Two at how anyone can wake up to the miraculous. I promise that with practiced intention and the help of the Spirit, a little digging can bring them to light in your life, and with them comes the opportunity to strengthen your faith and trust in God's promises.

Miracles happen. As Albert Einstein famously said, "There are only two ways to live your life. One is as though nothing is a miracle. The other is as though everything is a miracle." I hope you will join me in seeing that miracles large and small are for everyone and occur far more often than we even realize. If we conscientiously work through our doubts and open our hearts to what God is up to, we'll see that the breathtaking realities of heaven are much closer for each of us than we have dared to believe.

Chapter 9

—

ANGELS WALK AMONG US

"Praise the Lord, you his angels,
you mighty ones who do his bidding,
who obey his word."

—Psalm 103:20

Remember the two Chilean men who suddenly appeared on the riverbank just as I was resuscitated? I am convinced they were angels, and now I'll tell you why.

We were in an isolated spot on the river, yet they did not come to the bank by boat, nor did they slash their way through a bamboo thicket. According to my friends who were fervently performing CPR, the men just appeared. One moment, they were not there—the next moment, they were standing among my friends. They were wearing clothing typical of rural Chilean workers—handmade woolen sweaters with rough-hewn work pants. Other than the fact of their presence, they were neither flashy nor unusual.

Without speaking or being spoken to, these men, along with my friends, began to crash through the thick bamboo to create a way out to the road above. Step by step, they bushwhacked through the bamboo and clambered up the steep hillside, all while carrying my body on a kayak used as a stretcher. After slow progress up the hillside, then along a small animal trail, our group finally emerged onto a dirt road.

As I wrote earlier, at the exact spot where we emerged onto the road, an ambulance was parked, waiting. Although he seemed to follow no typical protocol, the ambulance driver, as if fully expecting us, silently and calmly sprang into action at our arrival. He did not administer any medical assistance to me, even though I was fading in and out of consciousness and was clearly in distress; he merely loaded me into the back of the ambulance, walked to the front of the vehicle, and quickly began driving. One person asked the driver what he had been doing there, to which he replied, "I don't know, just waiting." Other than this, he never spoke. The driver appeared to be kind and middle-aged. Ambulance drivers in Chile typically wear uniforms, but this driver was wearing sophisticated slacks and a little lab-coat-type jacket. To my companions, everything seemed odd and out of place.

Once I had been transferred to the ambulance, the Chilean men who had helped transport me up the hillside seemed to melt into the scenery. My friends returned to the river later in the day to look for them but found no sign of their presence, and none of the local villagers knew of them.

Angels come, and angels go.

The ambulance finally arrived at a little medical clinic that had only recently been established. It was open only once every six weeks, yet it happened to be open when I arrived. There wasn't an x-ray machine, but x-rays were not needed to know that both of my legs were quite obviously broken—moving like a rag doll, the bones and ligaments around both of my knees were totally unstable on examination. My husband found few medical supplies inside the clinic, but he did find some plaster with which he was able to fabricate long splints for both of my legs before loading me into a pickup truck to begin our journey home. After I had been taken inside the clinic, the ambulance driver did not get out of the vehicle, but just drove away. No questions asked and none answered.

As I recounted in the previous chapter, I have been asked numerous times what I think *really* happened on the riverbank. Who were the Chilean men? What was the ambulance doing there? And how did Bill know where to go?

My answer is always the same: God intervened. After carefully considering all the circumstances and possibilities, I believe the kayaker who went running into the bamboo forest was divinely guided to where Bill was reading, and their perfectly timed arrival where we emerged was no coincidence. I believe the Chilean men who carried me away from the river and the ambulance driver waiting by the road for us were divinely sent by God to fulfill His plan for me.

And that's why I conclude they were angels—divine messengers on assignment from God.

I'll never know all the reasons God chose to intercede on my behalf that day. But I do know the outcome, and I'm deeply grateful. The writer of the book of Hebrews poses a most revealing rhetorical question. He asks, "Are not all angels ministering spirits?" (1:14).

In my experience, the answer is yes!

In the previous chapter, we looked at the evidence for the miraculous in our world. On that score, what heaven reveals is clear, and a cause for celebration: God is present and active in supernatural ways in our world—and He wants us to notice!

In this chapter we see that God often accomplishes the miraculous by asking powerful emissaries we know as angels to cross over into our physical world.

MESSENGERS ON ASSIGNMENT

Has your life been "touched by an angel"? Almost certainly. The Bible describes the multitudes of angels who wait at all times to do God's bidding among us (see, for example, Genesis 28:12, Exodus 23:20, Matthew 26:53, and John 1:51). In this chapter, I'll share stories—lots of them—that others have shared with me, and for an important reason: Waking up to the unseen all around us can radically change how we go about our daily lives. I learned in heaven that you and I are never alone, never unnoticed, never far from one of God's beautiful and powerful "ministering spirits."

Stories of angels pepper the pages of the Bible and are mentioned in the holy texts of most major religions. In heaven, they form God's praise and worship team in heaven (Isaiah 6:1–3; Luke 2:13–14; Revelation 4–5, 8; 5:11; 7:11). On Earth, they do the work of heaven as messengers, protectors, and comforters. I love the line from Psalm 103 (at the top of this chapter) where they are described as "mighty ones who do His bidding."

Throughout the Bible, angels suddenly appear and, just as quickly, disappear. They came to people in human form, animal form, and even inanimate form (Genesis 18, Numbers 22, Exodus 23). They can look like lightning, fire, polished metal, or precious stones, and they can appear as men or women, can stand, sit, and eat, and have wind in their wings.

Then, as now, when angels show up, humans are usually taken by surprise. Whether it's this element of surprise, or the sudden experience of a being of such great power, angelic visits in scripture often begin with reassurance. The heavenly visitor first says, "Do not be afraid" or "Do not fear." But uncertainty about why they have come is never an issue, at least once we've received what they have come to say or do.

Clearly, these "mighty ones" can speak to us in whatever way we will understand, and they appear to us in whatever form will achieve their mission (Genesis 18:1–19, Daniel 10:5–6).

Karen, who wrote me from St. Louis, Missouri, told about her desperate prayer to a God she thought of as far away. Then she "saw" angels near:

> *My body, mind, and soul were so crushed by the physical and emotional abuse at the hands of my new husband that I got down on my knees beside my bed, buried my face in my hands, and wept inconsolably, as I called out for what I thought was a faraway, unapproachable God to help me.*
>
> *Suddenly, outside my side window, I heard beautiful singing that sounded like falling waters, a waterfall gently rushing in a perfection of three male voices, praising God's mercy. I jumped up to see them and the voices moved to the front window. I ran over to the front window, wanting to see them, but couldn't with my human eyes. But I could hear them clearly, more precisely than any sound with my ears. I saw them in spirit—there is no other way to explain it. Their presence was large, comforting, beckoning me to drink of God's glory and peace.*
>
> —KAREN, ST. LOUIS, MO

We find many stories of the remarkable protection angels bring to vulnerable people—often but not always in response to prayer:

> *A young woman walking home from work in Brooklyn had to go past a young man loitering against a building. She was fearful; there had been muggings in the area recently, and she prayed for protection. She had to go right by him, and although she could feel him watching her, he didn't move.*

A short time after she reached home, she heard sirens and saw police lights. The next day, her neighbor told her someone had been raped, in the same place and just after she had passed by the young man. She wondered if the man she'd passed was the rapist, because if it were, she could identify him. She called the police and discovered they had a suspect in custody. She identified him in a lineup and asked the policeman, "Why didn't he attack me? I was just as vulnerable as the next woman who came along."

The policeman was curious, too, so he described the woman and asked the suspect about her. He said, "I remember her. But why would I have bothered her? She was walking down the street with two big guys, one on either side of her."[1]

When I was in college, a friend and I were clowning around riding on top of an elevator (not in it, but on top of it). Elevators in those days had a heavy counterweight (perhaps they still do) that moves in the opposite direction of the elevator.

We were on our way down and, for whatever reason, I had my foot halfway over the opening and halfway on the top of the elevator. I was not paying particular attention to it, but at one point I heard a loud voice say, "Get your foot out of that opening now!"

I quickly pulled back my foot and immediately the counterweight slammed past. Had my foot been caught by the counterweight, it probably would have been sheared off or crushed. I believe God knew that through running, I would be able to speak with Him and that He didn't want to take that away from me before it even began (my running career began about ten years later).

—BARRY, GREEN BAY, WI

One of the most vivid descriptions of an angel came to me via Facebook from a woman named Kelly. Her angelic visitation happened in childhood, but her ability to recall details of appearance and manner is striking:

> *I have been a registered nurse for almost twenty-five years, working in hospice and critical care. Ever since I was a tiny girl, I always knew that God was real. When I was ten years old, I suffered extreme physical and verbal abuse from my alcoholic stepparents.*
>
> *One afternoon, I was alone in my bedroom, sitting on my bed coloring in a coloring book. All of a sudden, I looked up and an angel was standing in the doorway of my room. He was very tall (at least seven feet) as he had to bend down under the doorway to look at me. He was so beautiful! He had blond curly hair and intense blue eyes. He was wearing a white robe with a gold rope belt. He had sandals on his feet. He did not have wings, but I knew he was an angel. He stood five feet from me, and he was as real as anyone. He was solid-looking, not transparent like a ghost. He radiated light from his skin and his beauty was breathtaking. He looked into my eyes with so much love, and he smiled at me.*
>
> *I remember this as vividly as if it just happened yesterday, and I am fifty-three years old now.*
>
> —KELLY, NEWPORT, RI

Unfortunately, we suffer from a few misconceptions about angels, too.

For one, as enthralling as it might be to imagine that good people become angels after death, there is no biblical basis for this hope. Psalm 8:5 makes clear that humans are different from angels. For another, it is equally clear that they work for God, not for humans (Revelation 19:10, Psalm 103:20). And finally, like all of creation, angels are under God's authority, and although we may feel a special affection for them, we are not to worship them (Revelation 22:8–9).

ESCORTS FROM THIS LIFE TO THE NEXT

Many who tend to people in their final moments tell stories of angels appearing. Sometimes angels seem to wait until the dying individuals are ready, but sometimes they arrive early, seeming to beckon them along toward heaven. Witnessing this can be confusing and frightening to family or friends, but more often the presence of angels brings comfort and a deep sense of God's loving, personal care:

My mother had been diagnosed with emphysema, and her doctors believed she only had a short time to live. Because of her deep faith, my mother experienced a very holy death. She was not afraid to die. In fact, she looked forward to joining my daddy and others who had gone before her.

My friend Sue would often play her harp, and we would all gather around my mother's bed and sing praise music. Once, Mother bolted straight up in the bed and said, "Am I dead yet? This dying is not bad at all!"

One day, Bishop Frank held a Diocesan Convention and wanted to bring Mother Holy Communion before the meeting. When he walked into her bedroom, she said to me, "Emmy, did you see that angel fly in over Frank's head when he opened the door?" I hadn't seen it, but she clearly had.

Frank gave her Communion and prayed with her. A few hours later, Mother called me into her room and said, "Emmy, do you see those angels in the corner of my room? There's a path of beautiful flowers on either side, and the street is lined with many, many angels." The picture was so vivid to her. As

I sat quietly by her bed, she said, "Emmy, the angels— do you see them now? They want me to go with them. I believe I am ready to go. Please come hold my hand and help me join them. Wait! Honey, call your brother to be with us." As we stood on either side of her bed, she said, "I am ready to join them. . . ." Then she quietly departed with the angels.

Death for my mother came gently, beautifully, and in the presence of the holy angels.

—EMMY, JACKSONVILLE, FL

ENVOYS OF ENCOURAGEMENT

Not only do angels comfort the hurting or dying, but they are also sources of great encouragement. The apostle Paul was grateful for the encouraging message brought by an angel, who assured all who sailed with him to Rome that they would arrive safely (Acts 27).

I have personally been told many stories from people who have received comfort and encouragement from the appearance of an angel at just the right moment, and this may be the most common type of story I have heard. Wonderfully, people are always left with a deep and long-lasting sense of God's peace and love:

When I was twenty-four years old, my girlfriend and I accidentally started a little family, so I had to drop out of college just before my senior year. I was working as a line cook and was miserable with myself for my recent choices. On one particularly dismal day, I was cooking on the demonstration line—an open line where customers could watch the cooks work—but I purposefully had my back to the crowd. I was thinking of how my life had gone wrong and how I had let down my family. I wasn't sure if I could actually go on any longer.

Then I felt an uncontrollable urge to turn around, right then. So I did. Sitting at the counter was an old man wearing a distinctive red hat and drinking coffee. He looked like a typical customer except for a huge smile and an indescribable radiance. I started to talk to him and before I knew it, we were joking around. I suddenly felt great! I was cooking like my normal show-off self and facing the grill, but when I turned back around, the man was gone.

The café was not a big place, and there is no way he could have left without me seeing him go. I was baffled and quite disappointed that he left without saying good-bye, so I asked the waitress working my section where the old man wearing the red hat and drinking coffee had gone. She said, "What old man? I've been here since opening and nobody has sat there all morning." She looked at me strangely, then said, "Just look at the place setting. It's untouched."

No way, I thought, he was having coffee! He was sipping it as I was talking to him. But when I looked at the counter, the coffee cup was unused and upside down. The place setting was untouched.

At first I shrugged it off, but I couldn't stop thinking about it. Then I started to think about the man's hat. His hat had said something—something important. I don't know how else to describe it, but the words seemed written upside down and inside out! Yet now I found that I could read it and feel it. It said, "Trust in God."

—DAVE, DENVER, CO

COURIERS OF WARNINGS AND GUIDANCE

Together with the Holy Spirit, angels often provide information and guidance, as was the case with their messages to Mary, Zechariah, Paul, and many others (Luke 1:11–23; Acts

27:23). Sometimes angels just tell us what to do, as they did when they found a wife for Isaac or when they told Philip where to go (Genesis 24:7; Acts 8:26–29). Sometimes angels appear in person or in a dream at night, perhaps because we are more open then to spiritual reality. Normal dreams are often confusing, but angelic visits are clear, leaving no doubt as to their nature or of the message they bring.

Every Christmas we remember that angels warned Joseph to leave Bethlehem and flee to Egypt to save the life of Baby Jesus (Matthew 2:13). Not surprising then that some angel stories contain a warning of some sort.

In her book *A Rustle of Angels,* Marilyn Webber writes:

Angels came to me one night in a dream. There were four angels all dressed in black. Even their wings were black because they were in mourning. These were not the glorious, beautiful angels I wanted to see, but I asked the one closest to me, "Why are you so sad?"

"We are sad because you are dying," the angel replied. "Unless something is done, you are going to die."

Then they were gone. Instantly, I woke my husband and told him the angel's message. "What do you think it means?" I probed. I was healthy and had not seen a doctor for four years, but my husband made an appointment for me to see a doctor right away. The doctor did a biopsy and a full battery of tests.

When I returned for the results, the doctor said, "You have cancer and must have surgery right away. You should be thankful for the warning the angels gave you. With the kind of cancer you have, there are no symptoms until it is too late." My surgery was on September 2, 1993, and I am still cancer-free.[2]

AN ARMY OF PROTECTORS

At God's direction, angels can intercede on our behalf and are sometimes charged with guarding us (Psalm 91:11; Zechariah 1:12). Angels who protect seem to use a variety of means to complete God's work, with varying degrees of visibility, as was the case when Elisha's servant could not see God's army of horses and chariots in 2 Kings 6. An angel actually led Peter out of his prison cell, and past danger, before suddenly leaving him (Acts 12:6–10). God sent an angel to protect Daniel from hungry lions (Daniel 6:1–28). And reports of angel intervention on our behalf continue in today's world:

A young lady named Myra worked in the inner-city ministry of Teen Challenge in Philadelphia. One neighborhood gang liked to terrorize anyone who tried to enter the Teen Challenge building, and they harassed Myra as well. One night, when she was alone in the building with the gang banging on the door, she felt she should continue to reach out to them with the gospel of Jesus.

As she opened the door, she breathed a prayer for protection. The boys suddenly stopped their shouting, looked at each other, turned, and left quietly. Myra had no idea why. Later, as the staff people were able to build relationships with the gang members, the ministry director asked them why they dropped their threats against Myra and left her alone that night.

One young man spoke up, saying, "We wouldn't dare touch her after her boyfriend showed up. That dude had to be seven feet tall."

The director said, "I didn't know Myra had a boyfriend. But at any rate, she was here alone that night."

Another gang member insisted, "No, we saw him. He was right behind her, big as life in his classy white suit."[3]

One day, Jesus motioned to children nearby and then turned to his followers. "See that you do not despise one of these little ones. For I tell you that their angels in heaven always see the face of my Father in heaven" (Matthew 18:10). From this story, I believe, came the tradition of guardian angels. After the Cokeville, Wyoming, bombing, many of the young survivors reported seeing an angel over each child's head.[4]

Many people have shared with me their stories of guardian angels. These sometimes come as short vignettes, containing few details. But short or long, I'm always struck by their almost physical certainty about what happened:

I was about thirteen years old when I was going upstairs to my room, pulling my entire weight on the handrail, when it suddenly came off in my hand. I fell backward, headfirst. Halfway into a terrible fall, I felt a strong hand on my back push me upright. There was nobody there—well, nobody visible![5]

One time when my husband and I went to Bermuda, I tried riding my own motorbike instead of riding on the back of his. I confused the controls and drove it full speed into a stone wall. Just before the bike hit the wall, I felt something like arms lift me off the bike and place me lovingly, gently, on the grass. Even though the bike was destroyed, I didn't get a scratch.

—TERRI, PHILADELPHIA, PA

A couple of years ago, my husband and I developed a close relationship with a precious eight-year-old girl. Her family sat next to us in church every Sunday, and she would draw pictures for us during the sermon. One day at school, she became bel-

ligerent, hitting, yelling, and spitting at the other children. This behavior was totally uncharacteristic of her, but the school asked her parents to take her home. A child psychologist diagnosed her as schizophrenic and admitted her to a children's psychiatric hospital.

As a member of my church's healing prayer team, I met weekly with the group to pray for those in need. One morning as we were praying, I had a vision about this little girl. I saw in my mind's eye a figure who I "knew" was the Archangel Michael. He was standing in the door of the girl's hospital room, guarding her. He was large in stature and held a double-edged sword slanted across the open door to her room, barring any entrance. His eyes were fierce. He was dressed like a Roman soldier, with a short tunic gathered at the waist by a leather belt. The "skirt" of his outfit was made of tooled leather strips hanging down to his knees. He wore sandals that were laced and wrapped around his strong legs. I shared my vision with my prayer group as we continued praying.

The next day, a friend called to say that the girl had been released from the hospital. She was perfectly fine and was back at school being the sweet girl everyone loved. Later when I saw her at church, she leaned over and said, "I have a new friend. His name is Michael, and he takes care of me."

—JENNIFER, BOSTON, MA

ANGELS IN DISGUISE

Sometimes the presence of an angel is clear and recognizable. Most of the time, however, angels operate undercover and don't draw attention to themselves. Perhaps a stranger has given valuable advice or assistance in a stressful or dangerous circumstance, only to later disappear.

Many people have likely interacted with angels without

being aware of it, while others may have had an inkling that a supernatural encounter occurred. As Hebrews 13:2 says "Do not forget to show hospitality to strangers, for by so doing some people have shown hospitality to angels without knowing it."

In the early '70s some friends and I met in a town about fifty miles from where I live for coffee and pop. We were talking in general about some of the differences in our churches. A man entered wearing what looked to me like a monk's habit and a rope belt. He asked if he could join us at the table. He joined the discussion and said that Jesus only asked three things of us: Honor God, Believe in Christ, and love one another. Everything else will fall into place.

It was dark and raining when we left so I offered him a ride. I explained I wasn't familiar with the area, so he'd have to give me directions. After a few turns, he said he would get out there, and I slowed to a stop. Curiously, there were empty parking lots around, but no houses or buildings nearby. The car door did not open, but he was gone. He was nowhere around—just vanished. To this day I wonder if we met an angel—nothing else makes sense.

—PAUL, LEXINGTON, KY

THEY WALK AMONG US

Neither I, nor the people who resuscitated me, doubt that God was present on the river that day. We believe that for reasons known only to Him, God chose to reach across the curtain to intervene. To this day, I feel awed and deeply humbled that I was ministered to by angels. And I know that I am among countless others who have either witnessed the appearance of angels or received their protection unknowingly.

I'm grateful that God was near, loving and active on our behalf that day, but I live differently knowing that angels walk among us. You can, too.

God cares. God is here. And his powerful emissaries are here, too, ready at a moment's notice to accomplish the work of divine love in our midst.

Chapter 10

GOD HAS A PLAN

*"Never be afraid to trust an unknown future
to a known God."*

—CORRIE TEN BOOM

If you were asked to name the most popular verse in the Bible, which one would come to mind first?

Go ahead. Take the test.

If your answer is John 3:16, everyone's Sunday school favorite, you'd be right . . . but only half the time. You see, yearly reviews of online searches show that another, much lesser-known verse just as often ranks number one. It's Jeremiah 29:11: " 'For I know the plans I have for you,' " declares the Lord, " 'plans to prosper you and not to harm you, plans to give you hope and a future.' "

I find this little fact revealing because it shows what people most want to know and remember about God's intentions toward us. In John's gospel, I learn that *God loves me*. In Jeremiah, it's that *God has a plan for me*. Both are exceptionally good news.

That God has a plan for you and me—one that is full of hope, purpose, and beauty—changes everything. Do you see why? It recalculates our worth. It calms our anxious minds.

It invites us to believe and act on the fact that we matter—infinitely—to the one who made us. It reassures us that no matter what heartache we might be feeling today, our future is in good hands!

Especially after my kayaking accident and the spiritual experience that followed, I leaned heavily on Jeremiah 29:11. In the months and years afterward, I struggled to find the courage to follow God's plan related to my NDE. I knew that what had happened was more than just my story—it was my story *to share*. For me, that was the hardest part. That's where Jeremiah 29:11 came in. It reassured me that God's plan for me was personal, intended for my blessing, and full of hope . . . and that made all the difference.

It's not hard to understand why Jeremiah's message continues to resonate so strongly. We're all trying to find our way in a chaotic world of war, deprivation, disease, and injustice. In our personal lives, most of us face painful losses that just don't make sense. Oh, how much our hearts long for comfort, for clarity, for reassurance that God *does* love us and that he's still in charge!

In the preceding chapters I've told you how my NDE opened up my understandings of God's plan as it relates to death and dying, angels and miracles. For the rest of this book, everything you read will try to answer the question, "But so what?" What could my story about the realities of the supernatural all around us actually change in *your* life?

In this chapter, we'll look at a question we face many times during our life: *If God does have a plan for me in all this mess, what is it and how can I find it?*

MAKING GOD'S PROMISES PERSONAL

What I love the most about Jeremiah 29:11 is that it not only portrays the heart of God toward humanity, but it clearly portrays the heart of God toward me, individually. These are His plans for *me*. This is His desire for *my* life. And of course the same is true for *you*. God longs for each of us to live with hope and joy.

But is that too good to be true? At first, I found myself wondering if I might be stealing someone else's promise. Here's what I mean: As beloved as these words from God are for Bible lovers, some theologians warn against applying them to our own life. Some point out that the conversation God is having with the prophet Jeremiah is specifically about and for the exiled people of Judah. Others warn against believing God has a personal plan for each of us.

I invite you to work through this objection carefully with me. If you do, I think you'll see as I did why those opinions don't add up.

Bible verses are our most trusted source of understanding God's nature, His desires, and His expectations for us. We routinely personalize the words, actions, parables, and stories of the Bible as we look for guidance and direction in our thoughts and actions. Why? Because if biblical promises speak to God's nature, then they are not limited to a specific time, place, or person. If we are God's beloved children and biblical promises reflect God's nature, then it only makes sense to apply biblical promises to our own lives. When God reveals Himself and His nature to one person, He does so for all people, and forever. Times change, but God doesn't. That's why I believe we can bring our own experiences, fears, and hopes to scripture with the expectation that we, too, will meet God in the now. Doing just that has kept Scripture relevant, applicable, and meaningful to every generation.

So many examples come to mind. Take Psalm 23, another top-ten choice among scripture favorites. We could all agree that David is really speaking about himself in these passages because he uses the first-person pronoun when he writes:

> *"The Lord is my shepherd. I lack nothing.*
> *He makes me lie down in green pastures,*
> *he leads me beside quiet waters,*
> *he refreshes my soul. . . .*
> *Surely your goodness and love will follow me*
> *all the days of my life,*
> *and I will dwell in the house of the Lord forever."*

Should the truths revealed in David's lovely poem stay locked in the past? Of course not. He never mentioned me, or you, or anyone else, but throughout the twenty-five centuries since David first wrote those words, these truths have continued to be available for all those who are facing persecution, abandonment, war, and disease. They have continued to offer comfort for people facing a rocky relationship, a bad day at the office, or any one of a myriad of struggles. Generations of believers have agreed that David's declarations are not limited to person or place, but reflect the nature of our unchanging God. With deep gratitude, I can claim these words for myself and my life, as can each of you.

Or consider New Testament letters that were written to specific groups of people. For example, Paul's encouragement to a church in Greece: "Do not be anxious about anything, but in every situation, by prayer and petition, with thanksgiving, present your requests to God. And the peace of God, which transcends all understanding, will guard your hearts and your minds in Christ Jesus" (Philippians 4:6–7). Or those he wrote to believers in what is modern-day Turkey: "For it is by grace you have been saved, through faith—and this is not from yourselves, it is the gift of God" (Ephesians 2:8). Think how the life-changing truths captured in these verses have brought light and hope to people throughout the world in the many centuries since they were actually written!

Another of today's most popular Bible verses is Joshua 1:9: "Have I not commanded you? Be strong and courageous. Do not be afraid; do not be discouraged, for the Lord your God will be with you wherever you go." Although these words were spoken directly to Joshua after the death of Moses, they remain true in every single detail. Why shouldn't we claim this promise of God's presence for ourselves today?

Even the Ten Commandments given to Moses begin with the personal pronoun "you." In Deuteronomy 5, Moses clearly states that the Lord's covenant was not with the ancestors of Israel, but specifically with those who were alive and present on the day Moses addressed them.

Not one of us was present on that day to hear Moses's words, and most Christians cannot claim to be Philippians, Ephesians, or even Israelites. But the Spirit invites us in each moment, as it has for millennia, to open the pages of scripture to hear truth for ourselves today. The teachings, stories, parables, and the love of God we find there speak to all of us. They are more than situational; they are universal and time-less.

That's why I can say with confidence that God's words apply to *all* of His people in all eras when He declares, "For I know the plans I have for you, plans to prosper you and not to harm you, plans to give you hope and a future."

HOW TO DISCERN GOD'S PLAN

But if God has a great plan for us, how can we know what it is? Many have told me they're not sure how to know if God is calling, or where He is leading. I get it. After all, we don't get a full set of customized instructions in the mail.

Fortunately, all of us can find out what a truly faithful and God-centered life looks like through the teachings of scripture and the natural law we see at work in creation. In the lives of Jesus and so many of the saints, we are blessed with inspiring examples of the kind of life we're called to live.

Still, we often feel confused when we come to the crossroads of facing decisions, large or small. Especially at those times, we desire to know what God's will for us actually is, and we long for Him to take our hand and lead us in the right direction. Christian singer and songwriters Regi Stone and Christy Sutherland perfectly captured this sentiment when they wrote the song "Be Everything":

> *"I will follow you wherever you lead.*
> *If I lose sight of the path,*
> *be the road that takes me back."*

You might wonder more specifically, however, what this sort of leading might look like in daily life. While it can certainly be different for different people, let me walk you through this process as it works best in my life.

For me, the first step in discerning God's plan is to constantly listen with an open heart. Even when I think I am going in the right direction and doing what God would have me be doing, I constantly try to sense where the Holy Spirit is leading. I pay attention to intuition and strong feelings of prompting or revelation. Sometimes this prompting is more of a quiet whisper deep inside, although other times it can come through a dream or vision, as it has for so many people throughout the generations. I consider this stage as being one of active waiting; it begins with my asking for God's direction, listening for His leading, and continually evaluating my circumstances. When doors close, I look for windows that open, remembering that prompting from God will always be consistent with biblical teaching, and almost always involve service.

I always try to notice opportunities that arise, especially ones that unexpectedly grab my interest or do so more than once, particularly if it happens in different settings. When my attention is drawn to an opportunity, I ask myself whether it is merely piquing my curiosity, or whether it might be a prompting from God. If it's just my curiosity at work, the opportunity tends to be quickly forgotten. If an opportunity continues to tickle my thoughts, I give it more attention. I look for whether the details of an opportunity begin to easily fall into place, seeming to pave the path before me. Like others, I find that when I am going in the right direction, God straightens the path. When we are going in our own direction, the path is more likely to feel convoluted and filled with struggle.

I also question whether an opportunity might test my status quo, since God's plans often challenge our feelings of comfort and contentment. By challenging our comfort zone, the journey almost always leads to personal growth, greater love, service to others, and a future that is often better than what we might have imagined for ourselves.

I ask whether I feel an inner nudge or prompt. For more context here, take another look at the sections in Chapter 8 where we look at how God uses spiritual prompts, or even a brush with an angel, to give us direction. God has so many ways to move us along his path.

Most of the time, the feeling of being prompted fades away, but often the prompt becomes obvious, and God's plan becomes clear—not the whole plan, but the direction in which I should go. I then take a step forward in faith, all the while looking for confirmation that I trust will come along the path. I know that if I am actively walking the line of God's path for me, I am likely to find evidence that He is there with me, making things happen and pointing the way forward.

A pastor told me recently he had been offered a job position in a faraway town where he always wanted to live. He felt the time was right and thought this was a prompting of the Holy Spirit, but he sought confirmation. He paused and looked for God's signposts. Several days later, his wife mentioned, unprompted, that she would be open to moving. In fact, she told him she would not be opposed to moving to the very city where he had been offered a job. In her willingness, he saw a signpost of confirmation. They tentatively put their house on the market and, as further confirmation, received a full-price offer for their home on the first day by the first prospective buyer.

If no confirmation is forthcoming, the direction may need to change. It is like playing the game of "Hot and Cold": After the giver hides a gift, the recipient begins walking in their chosen direction. The giver then declares that the recipient is hot, cold, hotter, or colder depending on whether or not their path will lead to the hidden gift.

Sometimes the confirmation may come after the fact. This year when I was in Chile kayaking, I felt a nudge to paddle again on the Fuy River. I immediately wanted to disregard the nudge, as I had for many previous years. After all, this was the river where I drowned, and although the experience was one of God's greatest gifts to me, I didn't intend to repeat it. It helped that we would be kayaking downstream from where I had been so many years earlier, but it was the same river. I had never wanted to return to this river yet as I prayed, I was surprised to feel a growing sense of peace and confidence that the time had come to return.

The appointed day arrived, and I was extremely focused and alert as I paddled through the rapids. Despite believing that I was in the right place, it was a very emotionally intense experience for me. But with each paddle stroke I experienced an overwhelming sense of gratitude for the gift of it all. I even heard Chad, paddling nearby, humming "Amazing Grace." By the time I reached the end of the rapids, all I could do was cry.

When I returned to the house, I told my good friend about my experience and she told me hers. Instead of going on the river with us that morning, she had gone to Mass. Knowing the significance of my plans for the day, she decided to pray for me, and as she prayed, she heard a voice clearly say, "I was with her then, and I am with her now."

Once an opportunity, direction, action, or feeling catches my attention, I question whether it is a reflection of my own desires, or whether it could be a prompting of the Holy Spirit. I ruminate on whether it is actually a signpost of God's desire and plan for my life, or if it is just something I want to do. I step back to ask whether the prompting is meant for me, or might be intended for someone else.

On this point, don't worry what some spiritually high-minded folks might tell you. Thoughtful reflection isn't the same thing as a lack of faith or unwillingness to follow God's leading. It's simple prudence. It's you doing your part while God does His.

Jesus encouraged us to carefully evaluate situations and plans when he said, "Watch out for false prophets. They come to you in sheep's clothing, but inwardly are ferocious wolves. By their fruit you will recognize them. Do people pick grapes from thornbushes, or figs from thistles? Likewise, every good tree bears good fruit, but a bad tree bears bad fruit. . . . Thus, by their fruit you will recognize them" (Matthew 7:15–20). And Paul advised believers to test our thoughts in order to discern the will of God and know what is good and acceptable (Romans 12:2).

As a sort of quality checklist, I always ask myself the following questions before embarking on something new or different that I think might be a prompting from the Holy Spirit:

- Does it lead to a greater focus on God?
- Does it glorify God or man?
- Does it inspire and benefit others? (Even God's most individualized plans almost always involve our serving and reflecting His love to others.)
- Does the experience lead to greater love?
- Does it encourage, challenge, and develop my spiritual life, or that of others?
- Does it further develop fruits of the Spirit in me, or others?

By the way, this checklist helps when you're trying to assess the words, motives, and actions of other people, too. For example, when I hear stories of spiritual encounters or experiences, I always ask these questions. I look for the fruit of the story and see if it points back to God. While most people are honest and forthright, I am a skeptic by nature and am not so naive as to believe everything that people say or write.

EMBRACING THE HEART OF GOD
WITH OUR "YES"

Thankfully, we never need to fret about what we don't know. Our divine invitation is simply to stay awake and act on what we do know. After all, every insight presents a choice: Will I act on what I now know to be true, or won't I? Believing that God's plan for me is good, and filled with hope, doesn't change much about my life if I don't say yes to it!

THE SIXTH LESSON THAT HEAVEN REVEALS

God has a plan for each of us—full of hope, purpose, and beauty—and He wants us to discover it.

After my NDE, I found it easier to say yes to God's presence, to His love, and to His blessings. I'm sure by now you can see why. I had discovered for myself that with God at the center, life could be a great joy-filled adventure. I could live now, fully present in this moment, but also have a confidence that no matter what each moment brought to me, a joyful future awaited. Still, as I've said, acting on that confidence took courage. To trust God's plan and say "yes" to wherever it would lead me meant that I would also be saying yes to the challenges coming my way, including the death of my beautiful son and the daunting prospect of sharing my experiences with others.

But let's be honest about the human factor in all this. Even when we sense God's leading, and notice signs of confirmation, we can still continue to resist. Truth is, most of us are born geniuses at finding the many reasons to discount divine leading. You know what I mean: We say we don't have the time. We're sure we don't have enough experience, skill, or aptitude. We can easily point out a better candidate. Maybe we just don't have the energy.

But God does not necessarily call the qualified—He qualifies the called. (If you don't believe me, take another look at how key biblical figures felt when they sensed God's call—for example, Moses, Gideon, David, Jeremiah, and most of Jesus's disciples.)

I love the practical wisdom in a story from the Dutch missionary Andrew van der Bijl, later known as just Brother Andrew, who was questioning the importance for him of learning how to drive. One day, he received a visit from a man named Karl de Graaf, who was part of a prayer group in which people often spent hours of time in silent prayer. In his book *God's Smuggler,* Brother Andrew relates their conversation:[1]

> I went out to the front stoop, and there was Karl de Graaf. "Hello!" I said, surprised.
>
> He asked, "Do you know how to drive?"
>
> "Drive?"
>
> "An automobile."
>
> I said, bewildered, "No, I don't."
>
> Mr. de Graaf said, "Last night in our prayers, we had a word from the Lord about you. It's important for you to be able to drive."
>
> "Whatever on earth for?" I said. "I'll never own a car, that's for sure."
>
> "Andrew," Mr. de Graaf spoke patiently, as to a slow-witted student, "I'm not arguing for the logic of the case. I'm just passing on the message."

Despite his initial hesitation, Brother Andrew discerned that this was something God was calling him to do, so he learned to drive. Shortly after he received his driving license, a new opportunity presented itself—one that eventually led to Brother Andrew's delivering bibles and bringing the gospel to thousands of people in communist countries during the height of the Cold War.

Our challenge is always to trust God's path, even when it is impossible to see around the next corner. Brother Andrew later wrote, "That's the excitement in obedience, finding out later what God had in mind."

WHAT HOLDS US BACK FROM SAYING YES?

In the years since my kayaking accident, I have often considered why it is so difficult for most of us to say yes to God. When life is comfortable and satisfying, it is more difficult to say yes. But I've concluded that so much of our hesitation is rooted in fear—fear of losing control, fear of accountability, and most significantly, fear that God will change our life. We worry that God's plan may not be what we want, and we fear that we may not want to go where He leads. We fear failure, putting ourselves "out there," and we fear what others may think. It's an endless list.

Sometimes we just try to put our head in the sand, thinking that if we don't acknowledge God's calling to us, we won't feel obligated to respond. And our best future often lies in a direction we strongly reject—at least at first. You know the story of Jonah—when he got clarity on God's plan for him, he set out immediately in the *opposite* direction.

Personally, I had a terrific life before my kayaking accident. I had a great job, a wonderful husband, four healthy children, and lived in a beautiful place. I was very happy with my life and had no "issues." When I went to Chile, the idea of change would not have been particularly well received by me. I certainly wasn't looking for a new life challenge—having an NDE, then writing about it, then going public to the world as a faithful witness of what I had seen and learned.

Most of us want to know how we, or our life, will be changed by God's plan before we agree to say yes. We want to assess the value of God's plan, rather than trusting his leading. And it's just not in our nature to believe that God's very best plan for our lives might be *un*comfortable, that we might be put in situations where we're likely to fail.

No wonder so many of us wait until we hit rock bottom and feel broken to "find God" and say yes to the changes. It is during these times of personal strife that we see our real need most clearly, and finally opt for change. Whether we are at the bottom or the top, it always requires courage to follow where God leads—one reason I'm so grateful that God promises to help and strengthen us along the way (Isaiah 41:10).

Fear can be paralyzing, preventing us from exploring new activities, entering new relationships, and from realizing our potential. We all tend to focus on our weaknesses rather than our strengths, so we may not think we have the ability or the skills necessary for what might be asked of us. God rarely seems to ask us to do something we feel comfortable with. As a result, we may let our past failures define our vision of the future.

Or we forget that God delights in using ordinary people to accomplish great things. Joseph was a slave when he interpreted dreams, through which he saved Egypt from famine. Esther was a slave before she saved her people from massacre, Gideon was a farmer, and Peter was a fisherman.

Our feelings of being too ordinary to be used by God often coexist with our desire to be called to greatness. We assume God's plan for us should be spectacular. We want to be like Nelson Mandela, Billy Graham, Mother Teresa, or other great leaders. Few people want to be called to cleaning dishes at a local soup kitchen, driving the carpool, or clearing trash from a homeless camp. We tend to look at the end result rather than focusing on our efforts and letting God work through them. We imagine the joy of standing on top of a mountain rather than considering the work of climbing it. We forget that, as a Chinese philosopher Lao Tzu said many centuries ago, "The journey of a thousand miles begins with a single step."

I doubt Billy Graham, who created one of the largest Christian ministries in history, was thinking about his impact on humanity when, attracted by the controversy, he chose to attend a revival meeting while in high school. And I doubt Mother Teresa was aware of impoverished Indians when she was a schoolgirl in Albania. For that matter, I doubt that Jorge Bergoglio dreamed of becoming the 266th pope (Pope Francis) of the Roman Catholic Church when, as a young man, he was working as a bouncer in Buenos Aires, or when he was sweeping floors as a janitor.

Rather, each of these leaders chose to respond to God's calling by putting one foot in front of the other as God led them from one opportunity to the next. In doing so, they walked arduous paths of service on their way to a mountaintop. Most of us will never be called to this sort of greatness, and we may never summit the mountain, but we are continually called to take the first step. Without knowing where it will lead or why, we are invited to follow the path that has been laid for us, using fully the gifts we have been given.

Sometimes we may want different gifts or try to hide the ones we have, but we each have something unique to offer. Just as each one of the billions of people on this earth has a unique fingerprint and genetic code, we each have a unique combination of talents and gifts that can be used for God's glory. We need not fear those who can hurt our bodies but not our souls, and we can totally ignore the disabling lies told by the world around us. The one who is in us is always greater than he who is in the world (1 John 4:4). As we begin to walk where God is leading us, we often discover preciously hidden talents and abilities. We can be encouraged by remembering the words of writer and theologian Henry van Dyke: "Use what talents you possess: The woods would be very silent if no birds sang there except those that sang best."

STEPPING OUT IN FAITH

When listening with an open heart fails to make my path clear, I step out in faith and get to work. That's because waiting on God is not the same thing as passively doing nothing. As said by folklorist Doug Boyd, "If I have learned one thing in this life, it is that God will not tie my shoes without me." Rarely are we offered a sought-after job without turning in an application and expressing interest. It is impossible to see a beautiful sunset without opening your eyes. If my friends had not provided the hands to physically perform CPR, I would not have returned to life.

I truly believe it is possible for each of us to become yes people, trusting God's promises of being present, of having a plan for our life that is one of hope, and His promise of guidance and encouragement throughout our journey.

It's worth noting that God's plan is not always one of movement, change, or challenge. Sometimes we are led to green pastures and cool waters, where we can refresh our souls (Psalm 23:2). Sometimes we just need to stay fully engaged in our present circumstances. During these quiet times, we can still provide a window through which God's light can shine into the world. Our life, and our example to others, can glorify God even when we are bored at work, when we are doing chores, when we are caring for friends and family, and even when we think no one is noticing.

A few years ago I received multiple e-mails from a man who was bitter that his mother was slowly dying. He felt she had been such a godly woman that she did not deserve to die this way. He told me stories of the agony she was in and how he spent every day gently caring for her. He thought the process pointless and was relieved when, after many months of suffering, she finally returned to God. Without his being aware of it, however, his constant gentle care for his mother had been observed by a member of the housekeeping staff. That staff member's own mother was also dying, but was frightened and alone, as the two had become estranged. As a direct result of watching this man serve his mother, the housekeeper lovingly reconciled with her mother and provided tender care during her last days.

Seeking God's direction and saying yes to God's plan brings with it a sparkling gift from heaven—a joy-filled life here on Planet Earth. I know this from my own experience, and I promise that the same rare gift is waiting for you, too. The confidence you will experience as you fully trust God to lead you and make your path straight will almost miraculously remake your emotional life. Anxiety and worry will get pushed aside. You will be set free in new ways to express your God-created talents and passions.

Like me, you will discover the eternal worth of our own story.

Chapter 11

BEAUTY BLOSSOMS FROM ALL THINGS

"Death . . . is no more than passing from one room into another. But there's a difference for me, you know. Because in that other room I shall be able to see."

—Helen Keller

One Halloween, I took my children to a corn maze in a farmer's field in Idaho. A corn maze, as you probably know, consists of walking paths cut through a field of corn. Corn maze designs, like labyrinths, can be both artful and complex. You walk in at the entrance of the puzzle and see how long it takes you to find your way back out again. Of course, getting lost is all part of the thrill.

My family, brimming as usual with confidence and bravado, couldn't wait to tackle the challenge. We marched into that field of corn sure we'd come out the other side in record time. Our plan was simple—follow each path until we reached a dead end, then retrace our steps and try again, taking what we'd learned with us. Farther and farther in we walked.

At first it was fun. But after an hour had passed, and we still hadn't found our way out, I noticed a shift in the mood. By then we had lost all sense of pattern or direction. Hunger, cold, and fear began to creep in. Was this a mean Halloween trick, my kids wanted to know? What if there was no way out? Things weren't turning out the way we had hoped.

No matter how many paths we tried, we couldn't find one that didn't arrive at a dead end. That is, until an employee of the maze offered to help. He climbed to the top of a tall lookout in the middle of the field so he could see the whole pattern. Then he shouted directions. "Walk until you get to the next left!" he yelled. "Okay, now go about twenty feet and you'll notice . . ."

Gradually, relying on his perspective and guidance, we found our way out.

You might feel lost in a maze right now—and not at all in a family adventure kind of way. You started out with high hopes. But from where you are now, you see confusion, pain, loss, and disappointment in every direction. We all face difficulties in our lives, but I'm talking about the kind of heartbreaks that utterly crush us. When I lost my beautiful son Willie in a senseless accident, it felt like the light had gone out of the world. For a very long time, I didn't honestly feel that even the loving Jesus I'd met in heaven could bring anything good from such a pointless tragedy.

Maybe you can relate. If so, you know it's in times like these that we can slide into a crisis of faith. "Where are you God?" we cry. "How could you let this happen?"

In this chapter we tackle one of the most daunting questions any person of faith must confront: If God is all-good, all-knowing, and all-powerful, why does he allow evil in the world? Theologians even have a fancy name for it—theodicy. But most of us experience the question in deeply personal ways.

As I experienced heaven, I learned that within the fullness of God's plan, beauty really does blossom from all things. In the next few pages, I will share what I've learned and experienced, and what the perspective of heaven can teach us about suffering and loss that we might otherwise miss in our daily struggles down here on Earth.

LOOKING DOWN ON YOUR LIFE

Discovering that God has a plan for our lives (see Chapter 10) brings tremendous comfort on one level, but on another, it sets us up for some very hard questions:

- Does our heavenly Father take an active role in allowing, or even orchestrating, challenges in our lives? Or does He simply make the best of them once they happen—making sweet lemonade from the sourest of lemons?
- Does God ever change His plans? Can we mess up His plans for us by the choices that we make?
- Given God's divine will, do our desires or actions even matter?

If these questions seem academic to you, I'd venture to say you have never been crushed by life.

When I was rising up above that river in Chile, I saw my body. Looking down, I watched as my friends urgently tried to bring my body back to life. But my spirit was departing—leaving Earth for heaven. Already, I was seeing that frantic scene from a spiritual perspective. Down there, I saw fear and heartbreak. But I was at peace.

Today I understand that the only helpful way you and I can understand suffering is through a similar change of perspective. Down here in the corn maze of our earthly lives, what we think will happen often doesn't. Some hard things will just never make sense during our earthly journey. Instead, we must ask, What lessons does heaven teach?

If we do, and if we give God time to work, the logic of heaven often reveals itself.

I believe our all-powerful God both allows and orchestrates challenges, and He also uses them when they naturally occur. When Jesus was asked about the sins of a man blind from birth, He said the man had done nothing wrong, but that he had been born blind so "the works of God might be displayed in him" (John 9:3).

Lynn died on an operating room table and had a near-death experience. She saw her sobbing parents in a nearby room, but once she realized they would be fine, as she tells it now, she entered a horizontal tunnel leading to a bright light from which emerged two of her previously deceased and beloved dogs. They were radiating brilliance from within, and she felt nothing but gratitude when they came running to her and joyfully smothered her with kisses. They accompanied her as she walked toward a light that she described as a warm, living thing that contained all colors. She saw many people, including her grandparents and an uncle; everyone glowed with an inner light. Before returning to her physical body, she was able to ask Jesus whether it was true, as her elementary-school teacher had told her, that she had been given a lifelong heart condition so she would have a cross to carry like He had. She heard the voice of Christ vibrate through her as He said, "No, this heart condition is a challenge to help you grow and stay compassionate."[1]

Other unwelcomed circumstances and events can result from our own stubbornness, poor choices, and mistakes. In the previous chapter, I shared my thoughts on Jeremiah 29:11, which says, "'For I know the plans I have for you,' declares the Lord, 'plans to prosper you and not to harm you, plans to

give you hope and a future.'" How can God promise these
things to us when every life is filled with so much struggle,
pain, and disappointment?

I believe what God is *really* promising in this verse is no
different from what most parents strive to provide for their
own children.

Parents throughout the world imagine futures for their
children filled with hope, love, satisfaction, and happiness. We
want our children to flourish and prosper. We yearn for our
children to grow up to be peaceable and honest, to have integrity. And because we see the larger picture, we set rules to
keep our kids from harm. We don't give them candy for every
meal or allow them to cross a busy street unaccompanied. We
advise against lifestyle choices we know will lead to sorrow
and heartache. And we look for opportunities that will challenge our children to grow, teach valuable lessons, help them
overcome fear, and develop their abilities and self-confidence.

Of course, as every mom and dad knows, sometimes our
children just don't embrace our plan for their lives. Sometimes they take detour after detour, creating pain and discord
for others and themselves. Still, we never stop loving them,
do we? We never stop looking for ways to nudge them back
onto healthier paths.

I think God parents us like this. Although heaven's desire
for us is one of prosperity, safety, and hope, God does not
make it happen regardless of our choices. He made that clear
in the Garden of Eden—no matter what His plan is, time
after time He lets us be partners with Him in what happens
in the world and in our own lives. We are blessed with free
will, but that allows us to veer off course, just as our own
children are able to veer off course.

My point is that you and I are capable of creating our own
challenges and struggles outside of God's vision for our lives.

Yet God in His profound wisdom continually intervenes to point a way back home. Sometimes his presence is as gentle as a familiar tune.

Not long ago, Henry told me his story. He had abused alcohol, drugs, and people and had spent time in jail. Shortly after his release, he boarded a bus for his hometown, as his mother had died. She was his last living relative and, he believed, the only person who had ever loved him. As he sat on the bus, he hoped that no one would sit next to him, since he was lost in his own thoughts about his mother and his childhood. His mother had been a godly woman who tucked him in each night with a prayer and a rendition of "Jesus Loves Me," substituting in Henry's name. He was unhappy when a man sat in the seat next to him, and Henry turned toward the window. The man began to softly hum a song that brought Henry to tears—it was the tune of "Jesus Loves Me."

Henry's life was changed that day by a stranger Henry believes was pointing the way back to God. Henry has been clean and sober now for more than ten years. These days, he helps others recovering from substance abuse.

Look at Henry's story from heaven's perspective and you'll see an important insight shining through. First, God's plan for Henry didn't fail. For whatever reason, Henry couldn't stay the course. Second, even when "bad things" of our own making overtake us, we are never too lost to be reached by God's love. And here's where the beautiful power of redemption is most likely to show up. With every struggle or failure comes a priceless opportunity for us to seek God, experience His presence, and grow in intimacy, faith, and trust.

When words fail, I use mental images. Here are three that try to capture some of the mystery and scope of God's loving plan for our lives, even when bad things happen to good people.

1. GOD'S PLAN IS LIKE A RIVER

Because I love rivers, sometimes I compare God's plan for us to the experience of kayaking down a long and diverse river. There will inevitably be turns, waves, and obstacles. Sometimes we'll be swept up by violent currents. We may even be swept onto rocks or over waterfalls. Yet during these most challenging stretches, our physical and mental skills will flourish as we learn to negotiate the challenges.

At other times, we'll find ourselves drifting through peaceful waters. During these stretches, we'll face not a single hardship. We can simply float, enjoying the warmth of the sun, passing the time enjoying the scenery, and watching for birds, fish, and other wildlife.

For every mile of the river, our choices will directly influence our enjoyment of the journey. How we navigate a difficult part of this river can lead to satisfaction and fun, or misery and injury. We get to choose. Fortunately, even when we make poor choices, the current never ceases pulling us onward, carrying us toward our destination.

2. GOD'S PLAN IS LIKE A COWRITTEN BOOK

Another way of understanding God's plan in our lives is to liken it to an exhilarating but incomplete book. It has a beginning and an ending. It has a title, an introduction, and many chapter headings, but throughout, empty pages remain for us to write.

Everyone born will someday die, just as a book has a first chapter and a last. But I do not believe the details of our passage through life are all predetermined. If they were, it would defeat the very purpose of our soul's journey on Earth. We would have no responsibility for our choices and actions, and we would have no opportunity to develop greater love, joy, peace, patience, kindness, goodness, faithfulness, gentleness, self-control, compassion, and humility. Without being able to grow spiritually, or help others do so, what would be the point of an earthly journey?

Paul suggests that we have a role to play in the greater destinies planned for us by God: "For we are His workmanship, created in Christ Jesus for good works, which God prepared beforehand, that we should walk in them" (Ephesians 2:10, English Standard Version). Notice that he uses the word *should,* not *will.* Don't miss the "blank pages" in Paul's description! What God has prepared is still left to you and me to live out.

As our choices, actions, and responses to challenges begin to fill in the pages of our personal biography, each chapter comes to life. When we experience loss, the words we write for a season may be sorrowful or bitter. When we experience love, our words are likely to jump off the pages with excitement and passion.

The book belongs to God, but what ends up on the pages depends on us.

3. GOD'S PLAN IS LIKE A HANDWOVEN RUG

It's one thing to say that we get to participate in God's plan for our lives, but what if we make a mistake? What happens then? Are we derailed from ever experiencing the fullness of God's Plan A for our lives? Are we forever doomed to live out Plan B (or C or D)?

This brings us to my third image of God's personal plan for us. In the traditional process of making a Persian rug in

Persia, the rug is put up vertically on a frame and little boys, sitting on planks at various levels, work on the wrong side of it. The artist stands on the right side of the rug—the beautiful side that will be seen and used by all. The artist shouts his instructions to the boys on the other side, but sometimes a boy will make a mistake in the rug. Quite often, the artist does not make the little boy take out the wrong color; if he is a great enough artist, he weaves the mistake into the pattern and the mistake enriches and becomes integral to the finished rug.[2]

To me, the little scene of a weaver and a boy at work beautifully captures God's ability to transform mistakes and tragedies into a work of great art. It describes how God works in good and bad and addresses the problem of errors, failures, and even tragedies—whether of our own making, or by outside forces.

The year after my son was killed, I was skiing in the backcountry when I fell and broke my ankle. For several hours, I had to painfully ski myself back to our car. My ankle required surgical stabilization and kept me out of work. God didn't entice me into the backcountry or cause me to break my ankle, but He was certainly able to turn my mistake into a beautiful gift—breaking my ankle directly led to my meeting Father Ubald, a Rwandan priest whose presence in our home helped dissolve the deep feeling of despair that permeated my family after the loss of our son.

Our Creator God is always at work in the fabric of our lives, weaving the details—whether lovely or ugly, carefully crafted or unwanted outcomes—into a wondrous creation, one where a beauty we could never imagine is the end result.

WHEN "BAD THINGS" BECOME "GOOD"

The overarching truth is that life confronts us with many daunting situations, many of which are later revealed to be blessings in disguise. Let me share some stories that I think you'll find encouraging.

Angie is grateful for the blessing of preparation she received, although she didn't appreciate it at the time. She told me:

> *"I had a near drowning when I went whitewater rafting while visiting my son in New Zealand. I experienced the most incredible state of peace while I was sitting cross-legged on the bottom of the river and being held there by the pounding falls we had just gone over. I wasn't even afraid. To make a long story short, my son drowned on the same river approximately one week later. Although I was initially flooded with agonizing thoughts about how my son must have suffered, God immediately brought comfort to me by reminding me of the peace and comfort that I had felt during my own near-drowning experience."*

My friend Jessica had lived a charmed life. She had a delightful childhood, an easy time at school, and many close friendships. She completed her undergraduate degree in three years and had been accepted into a postgraduate program when things seemed to veer off course. Within a month her beloved grandmother was diagnosed with cancer, and the summer job she had lined up was abruptly given to someone else. Jessica, who had always carefully planned her future, couldn't believe how her life seemed to be spiraling out of control.

But there was more to come. The son of a family friend

had been visiting her family when he fell, breaking his leg in several places. Because he would not be able to travel for several weeks, Jessica's mother insisted she come home to care for the young man. As you can understand, Jessica arrived home filled with resentment at what she felt was a continuing disintegration of her plans. Then events took a turn.

Over the coming weeks she discovered that she and this young man shared similar backgrounds, senses of humor, and dreams. They fell in love and eventually married. Today, they have three young children, and Jessica loves to tell the story of all the "bad things" that led her back home.

The apostle Paul wrote, "And we know that in all things God works for the good of those who love Him, who have been called according to His purpose" (Romans 8:28). That certainly sounds wonderful, but we often cannot see how bad situations are working for our good. We can't imagine how a fatal car crash, lost job, terminal disease, or senseless killing could possibly bring a positive outcome. But what if our problem is one of perspective? We are looking at circumstances from where we stand, muddling through the maze of life on Earth.

Dennis had been a bricklayer since before he graduated from high school. At sixty-three years old, he suffered a disabling back injury and was unable to return to work. He was devastated, unskilled, afraid, and felt defeated. He didn't know how he would support his family. He shocked himself and others when he tried painting with watercolors during his rehabilitation and discovered his enjoyment of a previously undiscovered, but much appreciated gift. He went on to become a well-known regional artist with his own gallery, blessing many with his beautiful landscapes.

With time and distance, we're more likely to see the beauty and wisdom of God's plans, but most of us want to know the "Why?" of a situation now rather than later. Although Solomon wrote, "[God] has made everything beautiful in its time. He has also set eternity in the human heart; yet no one can fathom what God has done from beginning to end" (Ecclesiastes 3:11), we don't really trust that God always knows what is best. Sometimes, as with Angie, Jessica, and Dennis, the beauty does break through. But many of us won't be able to truly understand what our trials and tribulations could add up to except unwanted hardship and sorrow. That's because our perspective now is limited. One day, though, we'll see the complete picture.

RELEASED BY FIRE

Here's one more picture of God's surprising plan at work for good, this time through the utter devastation of a forest fire. Strangely, it's often calamity and oppression that give rise to the greatest transformations.

In the natural world, forest fires can be very destructive but also create the opportunity for growth. Majestic giant sequoia trees can grow to be three hundred feet tall and live for more than three thousand years. Yet to propagate, they must typically face the challenge of fire. The intense heat of a forest fire shrinks the scales of the sequoia cone, which may have been dormant for twenty years or more, releasing seeds that are no bigger than the tip of a sharpened pencil. The fire that releases the seeds also burns the leaf litter on the forest floor, creating rich, well-drained soil to welcome the tiny seeds.

I'm sure you see the parallel. Disastrous events in our lives can actually provide just the right context for important growth and transformation. Trust me, I don't like this picture of God's plan at all. Like most people, I don't enjoy change and certainly don't want change that comes through calamity. Yet I've seen that often the best, most healing changes in my life have been in response to heartache, frustration, loss, or setbacks.

In 1963, when apartheid dominated South Africa, Nelson Mandela was falsely accused and sentenced to life imprisonment on Robben Island. He was confined to a small cell, slept on the floor, used a bucket for a toilet, and spent his days performing hard labor in a quarry. He was allowed one visitor for thirty minutes each year and could write and receive a single letter every six months. As harsh and brutal as this experience was, it afforded him the time to deeply consider issues facing his country, including the need for forgiveness.

Without in any way condoning the suffering that came to Mandela and millions of others as a result of the racist policies pursued by the apartheid government of South Africa in his day, we can see how God turned this evil into good. Mr. Mandela's hardships sharpened and matured his character and abilities such that he could ultimately be the leader who defeated oppression, championed grace and forgiveness between South Africans, and helped usher in freedom and justice for millions.

Thankfully, emotional growth and change do not always require suffering, but it would be difficult to develop compassion without in some way experiencing another person's pain. I love C. S. Lewis's vision of a bird and an egg. "It may be hard for an egg to turn into a bird: it would be a jolly sight harder for it to learn to fly while remaining an egg. We must be hatched or go bad."[3]

In order to fly, we must first break through the eggshell.

Embracing the idea that God has a plan for us means always looking for His fingerprints in even our most dire circumstances. It means being willing to change our plans to match what He is doing in our lives. It means desiring His will more than our own. God has promised a plan for your life that is one of prosperity, and the true prosperity you are promised is the power to experience peace, hope, and joy, even in the midst of unwelcomed circumstances.

THE BEAUTY THAT COMES FROM ALL THINGS

God expects us to trust his promises to make all things beautiful in their time, but it is certainly not God's desire or will for us to become crushed by our circumstances.

I don't believe God wants us to be stuck in our circumstances of sorrow, illness, injury, or anything else that is not found in heaven. Often, he invites us to simply let go of yesterday's questions.

But trusting God should never equal passivity. We are called instead to reach for gratitude and peace in every circumstance, and act in faith on what we know to be true. Whatever we're facing today, however we might feel broken, our mandate is still the same—to share God's love at all times and with everyone we meet in our broken world. That's how beauty breaks through.

THE SEVENTH LESSON THAT HEAVEN REVEALS

In our mistakes and failures, tragedies and losses,
God never leaves us.
His goodness and love surround us.
In His time, beauty blossoms in all things.

My NDE clearly showed me the truth of God's promise that beauty comes of all things, and that understanding this truth changes the way I talk to my kids and/or patients about disappointments, challenges, choices, and so on. I am able to encourage my children to listen to where God is leading them, knowing that the plan for their life is one of hope and beauty. I am able to encourage my patients to see opportunity for growth and change during times of injury or disability.

While it is impossible to know what I'll be like fifteen years from now, I am certain I will be different than I am today. Between now and then, I know that I will continue to face challenges and will continue to grow and change as a result of them. This is one of the reasons I am able to experience sincere gratitude, and even joy, in the midst of sorrows and setbacks.

In this endeavor, you and I are never alone. A little like that man giving my family directions from the lookout in the middle of the cornfield, God sees the larger pattern where we see only confusion and struggle. He promises that as we seek His way, and listen for His guidance, we will find our way home. "Trust in the Lord with all your heart," we read in scripture, "and lean not on your own understanding; in all your ways submit to him, and he will make your paths straight" (Proverbs 3:5–6).

I know from my own life that, even in hard times, the comfort and grace of God's Spirit can enable us to live in gratitude for the ways in which we are being shaped, molded, and changed by challenges. That's why I can say to you gently but with absolute confidence that whatever heartbreak or challenge you face today, you can face it with boldness, knowing that each new encounter is an unopened gift to you from your loving heavenly Father.

Chapter 12

—

THERE IS HOPE IN THE MIDST OF LOSS

"And shall I pray Thee change Your will, my Father,
Until it be according unto mine?
But, no, Lord, no, that never shall be, rather
I pray You blend my human will with Yours."

—AMY CARMICHAEL

One evening when Willie was a little boy, I was chatting with him about some silly thing or another. I began a comment with the words, "When you are eighteen. . . ." I don't remember the point I was about to make, but I will never forget my son's reply.

He said simply, "But, Mamma, I'm never going to be eighteen."

I thought he was joking. Then, with absolute sincerity and purity of heart tinged with confusion he said, "But you know I'm never going to be eighteen. That's the plan. You know that." His words pierced my heart, but as I think back, they also prepared me somewhat for the conversation in heaven where I was told of my son's future death.

As I've spoken publicly about the loss of our son, I've heard from grieving parents who also experienced comments, actions, or premonitions that gave them or their children a

glimpse of what lay ahead. The story Louise told me one afternoon echoes many that I have heard. She said:

*I am in the medical field as a registered nurse. I, too, had a
child who told me at a young age that she would die young. I
took her to counseling at age six because, as a pediatric nurse,
I knew this was not normal. She wasn't upset by it—she just
stated it matter-of-factly.*

*In her teen years, she told me her death would occur in a
car accident, it would happen on a turn, and she hoped her face
wouldn't be messed up.*

*Last November, that is exactly what happened. Her best
friend was driving. Jillian was killed instantly, at age nineteen.
She had left notes for my husband and me on our dressers two
nights before she died, thanking us for being good parents and
teaching her about God.*

—LOUISE, HARRISBURG, PA

As you can imagine, the words I heard in heaven about
Willie reverberated in my heart in the years after I returned
from Chile. Despite the magnificence of knowing without
a doubt that God is real and present, that He loved Willie
deeply and had a hope-filled plan for us, the foreknowledge
of Willie's death weighed heavily on me. I didn't want it to
be true, and I prayed that God would change his mind. A
bold request, but even Jesus had once asked God to reconsider
His plans (Luke 22:42).

But how does my experience comfort *you* in grief, or help
you face your own death or that of someone you love? Nothing tests our confidence in God's loving intentions toward
us more than when tragedy and loss devastate our lives. Can
looking at our lives by what heaven reveals help in practical
ways then, even if it can't remove the pain completely?

That's what I want to explore in this chapter.

Mainly, I will simply share our family story. Certainly, my NDE prepared me in some extraordinary ways to deal with our loss, but if you've experienced a piercing loss and what comes after, I know you understand the power of story. In times of greatest need, we rarely need advice as much as we need to hear from others who are a little further down the road and understand what we're going through. We need to feel that we are not alone as we walk through this time of deep vulnerability, suffering, and hopelessness—truly one of the valleys of the shadow of death as written about in Psalm 23.

So, I want to share with you our family's experience and some of the wisdom we gained—and continue to absorb. Because what our experience taught us, and can teach you, is that when your burden of pain and sorrow feels too great to bear, the hope found in God's assurances can lift you from the darkness and bring color back into life.

A MOTHER'S SECRET BURDEN

In heaven, I was given a glimpse of what was to come, but no timetable for when it would happen. Morning after morning, I found myself waking up wondering if this would be the day my son would die.

I have been asked many times whether I told my son, or even my husband what I knew. For many years, I did not. Apart from trusting resolutely that all of God's promises are true, I sincerely thought this was too great of a burden for anyone else to carry, so I kept the information to myself for a long time. I continually prayed that God's will would be done, knowing that if the plan for my son's life did not change, great beauty would still come from it in God's time. But my mother's heart nursed a fervent hope that these things would not come to pass.

And even as I prayed daily that our family would be spared, I cherished every moment with these people I loved so much. I tried to be truly present in each moment, etching each experience onto my heart and into my memory. I tried to continually make sure all my children knew how much they were loved, and I made a commitment to never leave anything undone or unsaid. I did not try to curtail Willie's activities, but I certainly did not allow him to be reckless. Above all, I tried to leave no opportunity for regret in the event that God's plan for my son did not change.

The fact is, none of us is promised anything more than this very moment, so we should never assume there will be time "later" to complete something.

FOCUSING ON THE FUTURE

Years passed. As my son's eighteenth birthday approached, I began to realize the importance of telling my husband what I had been told. He deserved the opportunity to say what he wished, or do what he wanted, so that no unresolved issues would linger after our son's death.

I felt better after I told Bill, although I'm not so sure he did. We agreed, though, that the load was too great for a young man to carry, so I did not tell my son until the day of his birthday.

In the early hours of Willie's eighteenth birthday, 2007, I knocked on his bedroom door. There he was, sleepy but alive! I was so overjoyed that all I could do was to hold him tightly and cry. At first, he was confused by my emotion.

Then I told him everything that had happened to me and all that I had been told during my NDE.

He listened carefully. Did he comprehend what I was saying? I'm not sure. Willie was a sensitive, compassionate, and spiritual young man, and I don't know if he listened out of interest and compassion, or just plain curiosity. Maybe he thought his typically levelheaded mother was losing her mind.

Later that day, Willie had a brief conversation with his dad, in which he mentioned what I had shared with him. I never brought it up again.

In the coming days and weeks, I began to breathe easier, gradually letting go of the grief I had been borrowing from our futures. I truly thought God's plans had changed. For the first time in many years, I began to relax and focus on enjoying the rest of our lives.

OBEDIENCE IN GRIEF

I knew that writing about my journey to heaven and back was part of the mandate I'd received to share my experiences with others, but I struggled long and mightily against the idea. Finally, in the spring of 2009—ten years after the fact—I awoke early one morning with a compulsion to commit my experiences to the page. I rolled over in bed, hoping the feeling would go away. After all, my reasons for resisting hadn't changed. I still didn't have the time or ability to do it justice. I still felt that God had tapped the "wrong person."

After considerable wrestling that morning, my reluctance finally vanished and I said "yes"—yes to where He was leading me, and yes to all He was asking of me.

Two decisions in my life have been truly game changers

for me. The first occurred when I was pinned underwater, and I surrendered my life to God, giving up trying to control the outcome of my drowning. This "yes" was the second, even more difficult, decision.

That morning, I began a new adventure with God. As I wrote, I found myself thrilled to be reliving my experiences—allowing myself to be fully immersed in the experiences, feelings, understandings, and words that had been spoken. It was something I had not allowed myself to do in years. Some people relish their NDE and resist focusing on ordinary life again. I understand. Earth *does* pale in comparison to the vibrancy of heaven. But I knew I had been sent back for a reason, and I found that spending too much time dwelling on the glory of heaven got in the way of my trying to do the work that God had prepared for me.

By June 21, 2009, *To Heaven and Back* was done. As I pressed the "Save" key for what I thought would be the final time, my spirit soared. After ten long years of feeling like I had not done what God asked of me, the weight was lifted. I felt beyond exhilarated.

I couldn't contain my elation that day, and it was with this sense of total lightness of spirit that I drove into town with my youngest son, Peter. As we drove, we telephoned my middle son, Eliot, who was living and ski training in Maine with Willie, my oldest.

Their coach answered Eliot's phone and proceeded to tell us that Willie had just been hit by a car and killed. In a flash, I realized that the plan for my beautiful son's life had been delayed, but not changed.

You can imagine the shock.

"IF ONLY . . ."

I have been asked many times how I survived the death of my son, and if my experiences in heaven gave me comfort when Willie died. I'm not sure *comfort* is the right word. Like any mother would be, I felt devastated by his physical loss. I wanted one more day with him. I ached to see his smile, listen to his laugh, and smother him with kisses one more time. I sincerely thought the plan for his life had changed. I once read that when you love with all you have, you grieve with all you are. I deeply loved my oldest son—we enjoyed a very close connection—and I grieved deeply.

The trust in God's promises that I'd brought back from heaven certainly affected how I experienced Willie's death. I sensed an underpinning of joy, and an unshakable confidence in the beauty that was sure to come. But none of that protected me from the sadness we experience in loss. Sadness, like happiness, is an emotion triggered by external circumstances. I cried, sobbed, and played the typical mind games of trying to rewrite reality. If only I had telephoned him that day, maybe he would have been delayed by a couple of minutes, or even a couple of seconds, and the car would have missed him. If only he had decided to ski with his brother instead of going to his friend's house. If only I had visited him.

If only . . . If only . . .

Anyone who has lost a loved one in an accident knows exactly what I am describing. I felt empty and lonely and was filled with a longing to hold him just one more time. My husband shared these feelings. He felt guilty that we had moved to Wyoming. If we hadn't moved, Willie would not have become a skier, would not have excelled, and would not have been in Maine training.

I came to see that even when a death is anticipated, this

first phase of grief still involves temporarily managing the pain, shock, disbelief, and denial of the loss by mentally trying to rewrite reality.

Many days I wanted to stay curled up in bed, wanting only to be relieved of the pain, of existence itself. But I survived. When I was unable to walk, God carried me. I trusted that Willie was in heaven, surrounded by God's all-encompassing love. And even on my saddest day, the joy I found in God's promises never left me.

In the depths, I sensed I had finally landed on bedrock— the essential truths that would never change, and that could help me reclaim my life. I wrote out my "Daily Creed," attached it to the refrigerator, and read it many times each day. It reads:

> I believe God's promises are true
> I believe heaven is real
> I believe nothing can separate me from God's love
> I believe God has work for me to do
> I believe God will see me through and carry me when
>   I cannot walk

This initial phase of grieving eventually gave way to the long process of confronting, enduring, and resolving our loss.

I greatly missed my son's presence in this physical world and shed tears at least once each day for years, and I can still be easily brought to tears. I was no longer able to attend baptisms, funerals, or weddings because of the sorrow they stirred in me. I avoided grocery shopping, dining out, and public events for fear of running in to people I knew and seeing their expressions of compassionate pity. Although people try, what it feels like to lose a child cannot be fathomed by anyone who has not walked that path. Grieving involves mourning the loss of one's hopes, expectations, and dreams for a child's future. In a very real way, a child's death results in the death of the entire family, because its collective identity is forever altered. I grieved that, too.

Soon, the world moved on, but I still experienced my loss freshly each day.

PICKING UP THE TRACES

Willie was engaging, passionate, and inspiring, and our family shared in his passions. In his absence, the established patterns and dynamics of our family changed. Bill and I had lost our firstborn child, someone who helped set the tone of our family. Eliot had lost his best friend and constant companion, Betsy had lost her protector and role model, and Peter had lost his hero. We each faced the challenge of figuring out who we were now, and what our future identity would be, separate from Willie. We also had to figure out anew who we were within our family and what our family would become. Anyone who has suffered tremendous loss knows that this process is neither easy nor quick, and progress comes in waves.

We had planned the details of Willie's burial and memorial services together. Now, we worked together to establish a skiing award, as Willie was passionate about both skiing and the Nordic community.

He was also passionate about environmental stewardship, and our family committed to continuing his work by establishing the Willie Neal Environmental Awareness Fund. Willie had initiated a "No Idling" campaign which, on its surface, was an attempt to reduce unnecessary vehicular idling, but my youngest son subsequently discovered the campaign's true message. Willie believed in every person's responsibility to make conscious choices, get involved in important issues, and *take action* to make the world a better place. He very much internalized Mahatma Gandhi's quote: "Be the change you wish to see in the world." Peter helped us see that Willie's campaign had less to do with vehicles and more to do with life—not just about turning off your car's engine when you could, but about not idling in life. It was about embracing and making the most of the precious gift of life.

These tangible, Willie-centered family activities helped us find our way forward, and I definitely recommend them to anyone struggling with loss.

THE MYTH OF MOVING ON

The one-year anniversary brought some relief in appreciating that we had actually survived the year. But then came the second year. We were quite surprised to discover that in many respects, the second year brought even greater struggles.

By then, the "novelty" of our loss was gone, and most of the world had moved on. This was made abundantly clear when a teacher at my son's school responded to his metaphorical cry for help by telling him sharply, "Just get over it! That [Willie's death] was a long time ago." For us, however, the loss was still very fresh, and in some ways cut more deeply because the reality of our situation had permanently sunk in.

We were all so tired of being sad, but we learned that no one ever "gets over" the pain of loss like you get over an illness. It is possible to move forward, but it is never possible to merely "move on" and leave grief behind. Grief does not work like that. When a loved one dies, life changes forever for those left behind. A loss of this magnitude becomes part of the fabric of your being. Although a new life and new family dynamics eventually emerge that can be every bit as wonderful as the previous one, they are different. They can't replace what was lost. I liken it to someone who loses a leg in a traumatic accident. At the moment of loss, that person's life is forever changed. He or she will learn to walk and run again and will relearn how to create a full and satisfying life. But he or she will never forget the natural leg, or the feeling of using it.

I also learned that the way each of us confront, endure, and resolve grief is decidedly *individual* and requires a great deal of gentleness and grace not only from God, but for each other. Each person responds uniquely and on a different timetable. Most women respond differently than men, and children differently than adults. Sometimes men are consumed by guilt at not having protected their family, and fear that happiness may never return. In general, men tend to be less expressive than women in their grief, focusing more on retreating and resolving than on confronting and enduring their loss. Often children tend to reexperience their loss with each new developmental stage, as they begin to understand the loss differently. For example, I recently learned that Willie's loss deeply affected each of my remaining sons when they approached their own nineteenth birthday. Until then, they had always been able to use Willie's example as the North Star by which they could set a life course. But since Willie died when he was nineteen years old, they saw no course forward after that age, which left them feeling adrift.

In our family, because we each had different relationships with Willie and because he meant different things to us, we each felt the loss differently. The complexity of grief is made more challenging when a whole family is grieving, because the very people to whom you would usually turn for support are caught up in their own struggle. Often, they simply have nothing to offer.

For our family, that meant we could freely talk about Willie but found ourselves unable to talk to one another about our grief. If one of us was having a "good" day, no one else wanted to dampen it by discussing his or her "bad" day. Over time, this elephant in the room became larger and larger. I came to understand why people who have suffered a great loss move to a different town, change jobs, or dissolve their marriage. They think the pain they are feeling on the inside will change if they just change something on the outside. Or maybe they search for escape in drugs or alcohol. Unfortunately, it's not that easy. The pain of loss continues to resurface until it is fully experienced, embraced, appreciated for the love it represents, and incorporated into the present. This process is hard, to be sure, but necessary in order to move forward. (Therapists don't call it "grief *work*" for nothing.)

I also came to understand why marriages fail after the loss of a child. Certainly the guilt and blame some parents might feel at the beginning of the process can erode a marriage quickly, but I think many marriages just slowly dissolve into nothingness. Over time, a loss of this magnitude changes a person's view of the world, their future, and their priorities. But rather than talking about these changes and moving together in similar directions, it is much easier and less painful to talk about nothing.

Bill and I had made a commitment immediately after Willie's death that we would not become a statistic. We did not want to lose each other and did not want our remaining children to lose even more than they already had. Two years later, we were still committed to our marriage, but the emotional content of our relationship was withering. We were both still in so much pain that it seemed impossible to talk about our feelings. By then, the elephant in the room had become so large it seemed to crowd out almost everything else.

I considered counseling, but if you live in a small town, you can understand that finding the right fit can be tough. I struggled to find someone who understood the myriad issues related to grief, and also someone with whom my children would be willing to talk. Then, when we needed it most, God sent a small miracle my way. I "just happened" to bump into a colleague I hadn't seen for a long time. He knew of a visiting sports psychologist who experienced his own journey of grief after the death of his child. This psychologist subsequently met with my kids, with Bill, and with me. It proved to be a remarkable experience. Bill and I were having difficulty talking about Willie's death face-to-face. But with the psychologist in the room, our conversational dam broke. Speaking to him, rather than directly to each other, felt different and safe, and we were finally able to talk openly about our pain. We only met with him once, but the effects of his counsel have been long lasting. I have subsequently encouraged grief counseling to many suffering families, even if on a limited basis. Even one visit with a trusted pastor, friend, or counselor can change the course of grief.

WHAT WE LEARN: REST IN THE ARMS OF GRACE

I've noticed that regret and remorse are often causes of people becoming emotionally stuck after the loss of a loved one. Grieving friends and family members often feel a deep sense of disappointment and sorrow at the things they didn't say or do before the loved one died, or remorse for the things they *did* say or do. We are all haunted by those two little words: "If only . . ."

We often subconsciously believe that time moves forward

only for us—that there will always be more opportunities to visit, to express ourselves, and to make amends. After a lifetime of opportunity, we are stunned that the chance to ask questions, discuss something important, get to know each other, or resolve issues is forever gone. Some worry that their loved one did not know how much they were loved. Others regret not being able to express forgiveness, or to be forgiven.

The words Loretta wrote to me paint a piercing portrait of this kind of remorse:

I lost my brother nearly five years ago, and my grief is unrelenting. He suffered schizophrenia and had lived with me for seventeen years after both of our parents had passed. The psych meds gave him a quality of life, but I didn't know they were crippling him. I insisted he take physical therapy in a nursing home, and he succumbed to infection after fourteen months. I never dreamed he would not come back home.

I spend every day, almost every minute, thinking of him and thinking about better choices I should have made for him. Does my brother know how much I loved him and miss him? I blame myself and my stupid choices for his death.

If you find yourself pressed down by a heavy burden of remorse and regret, I certainly understand. Whenever I feel all tangled up in this kind of angst, I return to the amazing grace I felt in Jesus's presence during my life review. And I reach again and again for the promise he repeatedly showed me that God's plans for each person and for the world are plans of hope. God's spiritual offer invites us to put down what we did or didn't do and open our arms to receive His extravagant grace and unfailing love. Forgiveness is not just a platitude and God's grace covers it all. I have found—in my life and the lives of so many others who are hurting—that when we embrace God's heart toward us, we discover what we need to live with the burdens we bear. Only then can we discover the strength to make the most of whatever time we are given.

It's a vulnerable place to live—the place where our pain, divine comfort, and the fleeting gift of time so powerfully converge. I lived in this tender place for many years, dreading the worst, hoping for the best.

If that describes your journey today, I encourage you to do what I did.

Day after day, rest in God's heart. No matter what unfolds, know that you are welcome there. You are fully embraced by grace. You are cradled in the place where healing begins.

WHAT WE LEARN: JOY, NO MATTER WHAT

Many aspects of my grief were no different from those of any other mother who has lost one of her treasured babies. At the same time, I also had a very different experience from most of them. I never felt guilt, anger, or despair after Willie's death, but saying this does not make me special or extraordinary in any way. It only means that my time in heaven profoundly changed my perspective about life and death and greatly confirmed my trust in God's promises. I wish these same things, even in small measure, for you and everyone who experiences sorrow in whatever form.

Even on my lowest day, I remained full of joy. Does that sound impossible? I was certainly extremely sad, but happiness and joy are two very different feelings. Happiness, the opposite of sadness, is an emotion arising from circumstances. As circumstances change, so do our emotions. I might feel happy when the sun is shining, I have been exercising, my family is healthy, I talk with a close friend, or I have no financial anxiety. And I may feel unhappy when I am worried about something at work, someone hurts my feelings, my computer crashes, or I get a speeding ticket.

Joy, in contrast, is a state of being that is unshaken by trials or circumstances. It is based on a trust that God means what He says and that His promises are true. For people of faith, joy springs from an internal experience of an external, higher reality upon which we lock our gaze. That's why the first Christians who were imprisoned for their faith could "count it all joy" (James 1:2–3). That's why Jesus could know joy even as he walked to the cross (Hebrews 12:2).

I recently watched a major league football game, and I watched a player catch the football deep in his team's half of the field. As he began running toward the opposite end zone, he encountered other players trying to tackle him. He moved to the right, to the left, jumped up, spun around, and went through all sorts of maneuvers to evade his tacklers. Rather than focusing on these obstacles, he kept his focus on getting to the end zone. The touchdown he scored was his priority—his "big picture"—and the various maneuvers were his moment-to-moment circumstances.

Nothing I do and nothing that occurs in my daily life changes the eternal nature of God or His promises to me. Sometimes the circumstances of a given day bring me happiness, fun, and excitement; other times they bring me anger, sorrow, loneliness, or confusion. Regardless of what I experience during these individual days, weeks, or even years, I know that they do not reflect God's eternal plan for my life. It is this confidence, this absolute trust in God's eternal plan that allows me to transcend my daily circumstances and experience joy, regardless of my situation.

My joy is based on the certainty that there is a God who is real and present in the world, knows each of us individually, loves each of us deeply, and has a hope-filled plan for our life. It is based in the knowledge that every situation and experience on Earth is temporary. And every situation and experience is preparing us in some way for our future. As the apostle Paul wrote, "For our light and momentary troubles are achieving for us an eternal glory that far outweighs them all. So we fix our eyes not on what is seen, but on what is unseen, since what is seen is temporary, but what is unseen is eternal" (2 Corinthians 4:17–18).

HOW DOES IT FEEL TODAY

I know I'll see Willie again when I next return to heaven. Still, I miss my son's physical presence terribly. I recall the beauty of his eyes, his goofy laugh, and I wish he could be with us when we go on family trips and have new adventures. We all do. Some days, we ponder the future he didn't have, wondering what sort of husband and father he would have been, and imagining the ways he would have changed the world.

While time has not erased my heartache, my trust of God's promises has eased its intensity and allowed me to weave Willie's death, like all of life's experiences, into the fabric of my life. In fact, I believe my continued focus on God's promises rather than on my personal sadness not only helped me "survive" my son's death, but propelled me into God's plans for my future.

Novelist Eva Ibbotson wrote, "You cannot stop the birds of sorrow from flying over your head, but you can stop them nesting in your hair."[1] I never wanted a future without Willie, but I've found that leaning on God's promises during this journey of grief has prevented the birds from taking up residence.

The fact is, we all still have work to do. God is not done with any of us, and as we focus more fully on His promises rather than on ourselves, the fears that hold us back will inevitably dissolve. We not only free ourselves from despair, but we open our hearts to the joyful life God intends for each one of us. I found that during this time of loss, I was greatly comforted by leaning on the lesson that beauty blossoms in all things.

Every Easter morning, Christians the world over rejoice as we remind one another that death has been defeated. "Christ is risen!" we shout with hearts full and hands held high. What an astonishing triumph! What a celebration!

But how can we plant the beautiful truths of resurrection, the reality of heaven, and the certainty of God's unfailing love like seeds into the rich soil of our everyday lives?

Turn the page. In Part Two, I'll show you how to do exactly that.

PART TWO

Chapter 13

HOW TO LIVE WITH ABSOLUTE TRUST

"Trust in the Lord with all your heart
And lean not on your own understanding;
In all your ways submit to him,
And he will make your paths straight."

—Proverbs 3:5–6

I f you look carefully at every account of a visit to heaven or, for that matter, at any honest story about an experience of the supernatural, you'll discover a secret, very personal opportunity shining out from each one. You could call it "the right-now promise of heaven," and it goes like this:

If heaven and the supernatural are that close right now,
And if God is that real and that good and that loving toward me
   right now,
Then I can surely live more fully and more joyfully . . .
   right now.

Does that promise intrigue you?

If the "right now" promise seems far-fetched for you, it's not. But it is an all-or-nothing proposition. Both feet in. Your life and mine today can look radically different because of the reality of heaven. Or you can decide you're mildly intrigued by the stories . . . and walk away unchanged. If you walk, you would be deciding that every account, including mine, falls into the category of heartwarming stories—sweet, something you might even return to in the future, but not something that alters your thinking and remakes your heart and soul.

In this chapter and those that follow, I want to show you how your life can be different because of what you've discovered. I want to rescue you from a sweet but ultimately unimportant story time for grown-ups.

Make no mistake, this is extremely serious business. Today, I know without a doubt that this world is separated by the thinnest of veils from the next, and that both worlds belong to God. I know now that you and I already live right next to, even inside of, eternity, and that one day, the veil between it and time—along with all its schedules, clocks, tragedies, and eons of history—will vanish. On that day, everything that happened in time will be made good, right, and beautiful by God Himself.

That's what heaven makes abundantly clear: God's extravagant love permeates everything and embraces everyone and all peoples, including you and me—and love will definitely win in the end!

Every chapter leading up to this one has been my attempt to accurately convey my experience in this regard. I want to show you that the astonishing but true lessons of heaven are intended to refashion how we understand our world, here and after death, and how we relate to the divine every day. We could summarize them like this:

- Circumstances are seen differently through the lens of heaven.
- Death is not the end.

- God is love, and forgiveness sets us free.
- Heaven is real and grace abounds.
- God wants to be seen and shows His presence in our world through miracles.
- God has a plan for us that is one of hope, purpose, and beauty.
- In God's time, beauty blossoms in all things.

Each of these seven life-altering lessons we discussed in Part One are contained within God's promises that heaven is real and death is not the end, that He knows us and loves us, that He is present in our world, and that He has an all-encompassing plan for us that is one of hope. They are meant to change our way of life.

I call this transformed way of life, living with absolute trust. You and I aren't left here on Earth to simply press on in the *hope* that God is true, or even to cling to a correct *belief* that God is true. Instead, we're invited to lean wholly and confidently—in *absolute trust*—on God's unfailing promises.

Changing what we base our life on—from hope and beliefs, to an unshakable trust in the truth of God's promises transforms almost everything about daily life, yet most people avoid doing so. *Every* person is capable of making this transformational change—and thankfully, it doesn't require a traumatic experience like mine!

The wonderful news is that the promises of heaven are meant for everyone, and they're intended to transform how we live now in very practical ways: how we listen for God during the course of our day; how we welcome success and overcome defeat; how we make decisions; how we face challenges like the death of a loved one; how we approach our work, raise our children, interact with people around us, and pursue our dreams. And so much more.

Can you make this transformation without an out-of-body experience? Most assuredly, yes. You can wake up to the reality of God alive and active in your day, starting right now.

THREE STAGES OF FREEDOM

The universal starting point for this journey toward reconnection with the truths of heaven is found in that little spark of anticipation we all feel when we first wonder if God's promises just might be true. That interior yearning indicates that your heart has already opened enough to consider the possibility that God is what heaven reveals, and that His heart toward you is one of extravagant, enduring, and unconditional love.

I'm not talking about "getting religion," by the way, or embracing another Brand X spirituality. When you consider how many people on Earth profess to believe in all the right ideas, or who pin their hopes to some spiritual practice, creed, or ritual, *yet whose lives just don't change that much,* you have to admit that something is missing. Why are so many spiritually well-intentioned people stuck?

What's been most helpful for me is to rethink three common words we use to describe how we relate to God—hope, faith, and trust. These words are found in the sacred texts of most religious traditions. Christians cherish each of them, and for good reason. We hear them preached. We sing them in church. But what do the words really mean?

Maybe you've noticed—we use them somewhat interchangeably. Confusing things further, they can be interpreted so many different ways that we can end up not really knowing *what* we mean, or for that matter, *why* we can't seem to get unstuck in our spiritual experience.

By carefully naming—or renaming—how we relate to

God, I aim to help you reevaluate your actual experience and show you as plainly as possible how to access the new way of living that you've always wanted. I'm talking about hope, faith, and trust, not as theological terms but as *levels of personal conviction*.

Stay with me. If you look inside these words with me, I'll show you in very practical ways how to unlock the reality and power of heaven in your life today.

Let me talk about each level one at a time. For most of us, they describe a sequence.

We Start with Hope

Thankfully, most people on Earth have hope. Hope describes a feeling we have that if we just keep going, good things will come our way. Hope is like oxygen—we need it just to keep going. We express this kind of hope when we say, "I hope we'll have good weather this weekend." Or "I hope you do well on the test." Or "I have high hopes for next year." We are describing something we anticipate—maybe a lot.

Of course, the reason we hope for something is that, actually, we're not sure it will happen. When we whisper a bedtime prayer, go to church "because that's what our family does," or cruise through life believing that, if there is a heaven or a God, we're probably fine because we can always point to someone who's lower on our ladder of ethical behaviors . . . that's hope. Hope is nonspecific. Hope works as well for skeptics as it does for believers.

Ultimately, hope translates to "Maybe yes, maybe no."

But when hope is as far as we go in our relationship with God, or how we respond to His promises, then hope comes up short. Hope becomes more like wishful thinking than a life-changing conviction. We might feel reassured at times, but what about the times when hope fades, when we *don't* feel reassured?

Do you see what I mean? If hope is all we bring to the question of God, the reality of miracles, and the promise of heaven, we're not likely to change how we think and live, even if we want to.

That's why, as a word to describe a spiritual conviction, I think of hope as a place to start but not to stay. Positive feelings, a wish, or a longing are nice, but rarely solid enough to be transformative. A wish or a longing doesn't tend to last when the storms of life rage.

We Graduate to Faith

In my experience, the next step toward leaning entirely on God's goodness is one we often call faith. Again, to be clear, I'm not using this word in the rich theological sense so important to Christianity—for example, what St. Paul meant when he wrote, "By grace you have been saved through faith," or what the writer of Hebrews meant when he declared, "Without faith it is impossible to please God."

Instead, I'm referring to the way we tend to say and mean the word in everyday ways. Sometimes faith is as light and breezy as the advertising and political campaigns that declare, we just "Gotta have faith." A man or woman who votes in a certain way, or goes to church or recites the Apostles' Creed on Sunday, or simply checks yes to the "Do you believe in God?" box on a survey is said to be "a person of faith," even though this gives no indication of the strength of their beliefs or how they have incorporated them into their own life. Do you see the difference? As beloved as the word *faith* is to most Christians, Jews, and Muslims, what we mean by it can easily be confusing.

Is it true about you? Maybe you say the right things in church, read the Bible, pray, abide by a lineup of religious assertions, attend small-group studies, and believe that there is a loving God somewhere "out there." Despite your sincerity, you still live with doubt and hedge your bets. Maybe you can see yourself in the response I have often heard from people who are challenged about their faith in God. They say, "What's there to lose? If I'm right, I go to heaven and if I'm wrong, I have lost nothing."

One way I picture the consequences of living with this sort of faith is like this: It's as if we are pushing off from shore but only one part of us ever gets in the boat. We have one leg in and one leg out. We are partly where we want to be . . . but we're also partly soaked!

Honestly, it often seems to me that most "people of faith" are only partly "in the boat." The results are apparent everywhere around us. People of sincere conviction do not truly live the joy-filled life that God intends for them. Many do not reflect God's love or offer grace to others. Despite the best of intentions and desires, they live with largely unchanged lives.

When faced with real suffering, the benefits of God's truth, presence, and love are essentially lost to them. Their faith is shaken. How could this happen?

I think this is because many people equate faith to a really, really, *really* strong belief that God's promises are true. This is still different from translating that faith into trust, and it is the choice to trust that propels a person into the realm of transcending joy. For many, seeing themselves as "a person of faith" is as far as they go. Perhaps they suffer from tragically misleading information about who God is and how he feels about them. As a result, they're unable to take the step of transformation—and get *entirely* "in the boat."

That's where absolute trust happens.

We Change with Absolute Trust

Hope and faith become absolute trust when we personally see convincing evidence of God's presence in our own life and act on it. Our change of mind might come through personal experience, or a moving encounter with someone else's story—like this book. The evidence brings with it the realization that to live with anything less than utter confidence in God's goodness just wouldn't make sense. To *act* in faith on what we now know to be true creates a shift that propels us out of our old ways of feeling, thinking, and living.

We have entered the arena of living with absolute trust. The response of absolute trust is not based on emotions, momentary circumstances, convenience, or religious behavior. It is born of the recognition that no matter what happens during our day, God's promises are everlasting and unchanging—and they're for each one of us. This type of authentic, life-changing faith—which I call absolute trust—begins with a conscious choice, nearly always based on personal encounter, to risk everything on the unbounded love and goodness of God.

You probably can call to mind biblical heroes who made this discovery and let it change their lives in remarkable ways. Imagine how much trust Noah must have had when he embarked on his ark-building project. He was probably ridiculed while building it, scoffed at when loading it, and jeered at when climbing aboard. Once on the ark, he waited for the promised flood to arrive. And waited. And waited some more. He waited and trusted for seven long days before it began to rain. Without having an unshakable trust in God's word, Noah might have abandoned the project long before the floodwaters arrived.

Or imagine the trust of Daniel. He was cheerful, honest, and hardworking. But his colleagues were so envious of his success that they sabotaged him and got him put on death row. And then they brought in the lions! But rather than being filled with anger and fear, Daniel faced and overcame his circumstances with unwavering trust.

Many people hope that God's promises are true, and many more claim to have faith. But how many people have the trust of Noah or Daniel?

Only when we open our hearts to absolute trust do the beautiful truths of God's goodness really change us. And absolute trust is available for everyone—not just the highly religious, not just the saints of old, and—most certainly—not just the relative handful who have experienced a near-death experience!

REAL TRUST ALWAYS GETS PERSONAL

Call me a hands-on, feet-on-the-ground pragmatist, but I've found that so many of the grand truths of our life with God can quickly fade to abstractions. Belief and faith can be that for me. Of course, as ideas, they're no less important, true, or to be cherished less. But what I love about absolute trust is that it links immediately, directly, and predictably to a personal outcome. Real trust barely exists as an idea. If there's no action that leads to a different outcome for me, then I didn't trust. Just as grace is love in action, trust is faith in action.

Imagine you're hiking with me on a narrow trail deep in the tropical forests of Central America. We come to a ravine spanned by a rope bridge—the only way forward. Far below, we see and hear a rushing torrent. As we nervously inspect the bridge from our side, we notice it swaying in the breeze.

The motion, and the strange assembly of ropes and planks, makes the bridge look, well, *un*trustworthy.

But is it?

Without taking a single step farther, you and I can certainly *hope* the bridge will hold us.

Without taking a single step, we could even have great *faith* that the rope bridge will hold us—so much so we don't really feel concern about a bad outcome should we decide to march across the chasm. Still, we haven't taken a step, and we certainly haven't crossed the ravine.

Trust? That's different. You and I can't really say we have *trust* until we're in motion across that bridge. Trust begins when we make a choice and act on it. Trust propels us to take a step, and then another one, and another one—out across that sagging, swaying footbridge until we get to the other side.

That's why I say that real trust always gets personal. It begins with a powerful commitment that propels us in a direction we would have never gone without it. You and I can talk with great insight about hope and faith, but we have to *live* trust.

No wonder living with absolute trust in God's promises is so life changing!

For me, the emotional and behavioral benefits of wholly trusting God's promises continue to profoundly alter how I experience daily life. For example, I realize now that God's promise that He loves *me* dearly applies equally to the people I don't like. He loves the people who don't look like me or agree with me. Of course, I don't always want God to love others as much as I believe He loves me. That doesn't change a thing, though. He loves them anyway—deeply, unconditionally, passionately, and forever. He loves the people who don't like me back. He loves the people who have hurt me.

He loves people I think are unethical, immoral, or just plain jerks.

In fact, God not only loves them, but they are an integral part of His plan for the world (just as you and I are).

Trusting God's promises invites us to live in the freedom that comes from resting entirely on *God as he declares himself to be,* not on a god of our own construction. It moves us away from the comfortable platitudes and passionate songs that we mistake for being in true relationship with the divine. It enables us to transcend momentary circumstances, and to live fully the life Jesus modeled and God wants for each of us.

I care deeply about long-held Christian beliefs and what they teach us about living, and I have studied scripture, but I do not write as a trained theologian. Rather, I write as a faithful witness—an expert in only a few things, one of them being my own experience. On that score, I feel sent, humbled by what happened to me, and passionate about what I have to say about it.

My experience at the river changed me—not to perfection, I can assure you, but to something like freedom in Spirit. In trusting that everyone is important and deeply loved, I feel free to risk compassion for all people. Free from the anxiety about my own death or that of my loved ones, I've radically changed my response to death. When someone I love dies, I am certainly sad for the loss, but I also feel a small pang of envy, knowing the person is returning to our true home. In recognizing everyone has a backstory, as well as an ongoing story that God is actively redeeming, I am free to offer grace rather than judgment. In knowing that we all exist in God's loving embrace, I feel free to look for the loveliness of Jesus in every face.

This doesn't mean I like and enjoy everyone I meet—focusing on God does not turn us into perfect people, but forgiven people. I am, however, compelled to search for the beauty within each person. When my initial response is critical, I silently acknowledge my folly and forgive it, showing myself the same grace God shows to me. I then focus my thoughts on God's compelling and undeniable love for that person. I trust that he or she is part of God's beautiful plan for the world. I look for something I like about the individual, no matter how small, consciously softening my heart as I look for God's beauty within them. This tiny seed of connection almost always begins to grow, blossoming into love, regardless of how I initially felt.

Even when terrible things happen—as with the death of a beloved child—I know from personal experience that no darkness can hide the light for long. That is absolute trust, as best I understand and live it, and the payoffs for me or anyone are immense. "We shall steer safely through every storm," wrote fifteenth-century spiritual teacher Francis de Sales, "so long as our heart is right, our intention fervent, our courage steadfast, and our trust fixed on God."[1]

FOUR STEPS FROM WOBBLY TO UNSHAKABLE

Unshakable joy is built on the bedrock of God's promises. It reflects a trust in God's plans and the hope for His people. Most people actually *want* to trust God that way, even if the desire is hidden deep within their heart. Perhaps as a result, many spend years missing out on the joy that a spiritual life can bring, while searching for happiness on their own. But it doesn't have to be that way.

While many roads can lead to change, I will share a systematic approach that I have seen work well, even without the need for dramatic events. As you know by now, I consider myself a concrete-thinking, scientifically trained pragmatist. You won't be surprised then, when you see that the path to discovering absolute trust that I describe here is careful, sequential, cumulative, and evidence based. If sincerely undertaken, I believe these steps can help you transform spiritual beliefs that may be occasionally wobbly into an unshakable trust.

They unfold in a simple progression that we'll explore in very practical ways in the following chapters:

1. Look beyond. Open your heart to the truth of God's promises, and form a testable hypothesis.
2. Look around. Collect evidence from the natural world and from other people.
3. Look within. Collect personal data from your own experiences.
4. Form a conclusion. Reevaluate your hypothesis, make a choice, and act on it.

By following these steps, you will support your conclusions with experience and data, and with God's help, you will begin to live differently—with joy and confidence in His unfailing goodness. I am absolutely convinced that anyone can make this transformation, but it does not happen as a result of wishing or hoping. Each person must take the first step, and then the next, to make it happen.

I invite you to take your first step.

Chapter 14

STEP 1: LOOK BEYOND

*Forming a Hypothesis with an
Open Heart*

*"You have made known to me the paths of life;
you will fill me with joy in your presence."*

—ACTS 2:28

If you are honestly ready and willing to wake up to God's presence and purpose in your life, then I invite you to take your first, truly perspective-altering step in that direction. I describe this step as "Look Beyond."

To understand the significance of "looking beyond," picture yourself standing in a field looking out at the horizon. The horizon beckons you. It is the future you want—in this case, a life built on absolute trust in God's promises. But the field around you represents your life up to now. Since you've been alive for a while, the field is cluttered. All around you, you see obligations, old dreams, recent successes, relationships, grudges, disappointments, beliefs, memories—in other words, all the emotional and intellectual baggage that naturally come from a full life.

How do you "look beyond" all of that to the horizon where you can find and claim your new life? There's so much to distract, to hold you back, to argue against making any change at all. Your first challenge is to understand how you got here, then put yourself in motion toward the future you want.

Let's apply what this little scene suggests to help you begin your journey toward living in absolute trust. I propose taking three actions that will begin to free you from your past and present, and launch you toward the life you want:

1. Start with a self-inventory, identifying those things that have been holding you back.
2. Set the parameters for your search by asking the question, "How much evidence will I need to change my beliefs?"
3. Create a clear, testable hypothesis to give you direction going forward.

A hypothesis, as you may remember from school, is a statement that provides the starting point and focus of a quest. In advance, and based on what you know so far, you put into plain language what you think the evidence might support. Then you set about to collect evidence that will make the case for or against it.

Imagine what would occur if your search delivered such persuasive evidence that you could *truly* accept that God is real, present, and working in your life today? That He personally knows you and loves you as though you are His only child? Imagine the release of worry and anxiety you would experience if you truly accepted that God's promises and plans for you are full of beauty and hope?

Even if you approach this five-step learning experience with trepidation, I have great confidence in the outcome. In ages past, God "set eternity in the human heart" (Ecclesiastes

3:11), and without a doubt, my friend, you have eternity in your heart. (The fact that you're still reading this book makes that abundantly clear.)

Furthermore, you are not alone in the search—God is in it with you. And he promises to make known the paths of life to you, all the more when you seek him with all your heart (Acts 2:28, Deuteronomy 4:29; Matthew 7:7). That's why I urge you to bring your whole being—mind, heart, soul—to your search. Ask God to show you the way. If you do, I'm certain that His Word, His Spirit, His angels, and His loving presence will guide you to your true home.

ASK, WHAT'S HOLDING ME BACK?

Your first move in looking beyond is to take a personal inventory. I recommend starting with questions like: How open are you to seeing the reality of a supernatural, loving God at work in your life? What limiting biases or attitudes—personal "baggage"—might block your path or skew the outcome of your investigation?

A thoughtful accounting of where we stand now helps us figure out how we got here. We review our past, our spiritual story up to the present, and any previous conclusions that have shaped how we understand God and his amazing promises. Of course, we go through most days unaware of all this, but then at the moment when we most want to trust God absolutely, we hesitate. Baggage is blocking our way forward.

You could make your own list of what clutters your spiritual landscape (at the end of the chapter, I'll ask you to do that). For many of us, the list is a long one. Here are some of the obstacles others have shared with me, often through tears of anguish and heartbreak:

"I have been hurt by religion." Sadly, this is a familiar story. Many have become disillusioned with church and religion. In the name of a particular faith tradition, people may have brought more harm than good. An arrogant or hypocritical church leader may have inflicted deep emotional injury. Some of us suffered terribly from oppressive rules, silly obsessions, bad science, or uninformed and mean-spirited politics—all foisted on us in God's name. The perpetrators of this damage generally were not bad people. Even well-meaning people of faith can screw up the message of Christ. But in either case, the fallout is real.

"I'm not sure about the Bible anymore." Perhaps the scriptures, instead of bringing the good news of new life for all, were used in your past as a weapon to sow division, exclusion, injustice, ignorance, prejudice, or fear. Perhaps narrow interpretations of biblical passages represent God's nature and promises in ways that no longer make sense for you.

"Why should I trust 'the man upstairs' with my life?" Many of us move into adulthood with childish understandings and expectations of God. What might have been helpful or at least benign back then now saddles us with quaint, literalist, and patriarchal views of God that we reject. In real life, we need a God for grown-ups.

"But if I trust God completely, I'll never . . . I'll always . . ." Obstacles like these rarely get verbalized, but they lurk in various guises beneath the surface for almost everyone. We assume that opening our heart fully to God means that we will need to follow a long list of rules. We assume that we'll be limited in the fun we can have or be obligated to

do things we don't want to do. How would you complete the sentences from your own experience?

"I feel like I've moved on." Sometimes we can't separate the culture of a religious community in our past from what we feel and want in our present. As we mature, we don't identify with "that crowd" anymore, and we sure don't want to go back. Even the smallest memories—the unpleasant smell of the pastor's breath, the hunched-over old woman tending the church cemetery, an awkward conversation about our faith in high school or college—can stand in the way.

"I could never be good enough." I have spoken with many who want a spiritual experience but not the transformation that can follow. Others want to be transformed but resist the commitments that might spring from a deep spiritual experience. Either way, I believe many of us are held back by fear that we can't live up to what we think are God's expectations for us.

"I can't get past my intellectual reservations." Intellectual doubts get a lot of notice in publishing and media, and of course they must be taken seriously. But some people are prevented from embracing a deep spiritual life by a kind of intellectual arrogance. We allow our "scientific" beliefs to filter what we are willing to believe, or even consider. We claim to reject anything that cannot be seen, touched, or scientifically proven—ignoring that we routinely accept many unseen facts that can only be inferred from their effects (gravity, electromagnetic waves, the wind). We cannot see or prove the existence of love, kindness, or compassion, but who would doubt their reality?

"Religion is a crutch." It's the American way to view ourselves as strong, self-reliant, rational, and not in need of God. So often we want God's blessings, but not His guidance. We believe we have earned our achievements and don't want to share credit with God, although we may want to blame Him when things go poorly. Within our current culture, we value power and prestige over humility. It would be demeaning to our sense of position to wash the feet of immigrants as Pope Francis did, or to arrive on the back of a donkey like Jesus.

"I'm spiritual but not religious." Another common view in our time, this one assumes that spirituality and religion can be separated from each other, and that spirituality, freed from the limitations of organized religion, is somehow more pure. A kayaking companion once told me that he was very spiritual even though he wasn't into "the God thing." It became clear in our conversation that he, like so many other people who claim to be spiritual but not religious, simply wanted to design an experience of his own making—one that was not accountable to a larger community or higher revelation, and one that could be picked up or put down at will. Claiming to be spiritual can become another way to stay in charge, to *not* open our hearts to a power that is greater than ourselves.

"But you don't know what I've done." So many seekers I've met are effectively blocked from opening their hearts to God by guilt and self-condemnation. They feel they have done something unforgivable and, in judging themselves, believe they are unlovable. Others project onto God the toxic relationship they had with an earthly father. If you see yourself in this obstacle, you probably struggle with

deep feelings of being unworthy of God's love or of anything good happening in your life.

Would you say that the spiritual landscape of your life today is cluttered by any of the "baggage" I've just identified? Or by other obstacles you could add? I encourage you to describe to the best of your ability what is true for you. This isn't about finding a quick fix; for any of us, these kinds of issues are the work of a lifetime.

For now, I suggest you spread out your unwanted baggage in God's loving presence. Surrender it into his hands with a simple prayer. I could recommend this one based on the Psalms:

> *You are good,*
> *And what you do is good.*
> *Create in me a clean heart, Oh God,*
> *And renew a steadfast spirit within me.*
> *(Psalm 119:86, 51:10)*

Or it could be as simple as saying:

> *"Please God, take my cares upon your shoulders and give*
> *   me rest.*
> *Let your Holy Spirit help guide me, and give me*
> *   discernment so that I may know your love."*

I think you'll find, as I and many others have, that when we examine and name our obstacles, and give them back to God as an act of faith, powerful forces are released in our lives. We diminish the power of negative experiences to block our progress, and we give God room to bring the renewal we long for.

We are also prepared to take the next step in our journey toward our new life in God.

ASK, HOW MUCH EVIDENCE DO I NEED?

To "look beyond" constructively, we need to decide what it would take to actually put us in motion. For each of us, the approach is likely to vary. As a concrete and linear thinker, I expect integration of my thoughts, words, and behavior. I prefer data to abstractions, action to ambivalence. I am rather intolerant of hypocrisy. I feel that a person should intellectually and methodically evaluate religious and spiritual truths to the best of his or her ability, and then make a choice. Life's too short to dither and debate. On the other hand, once the choice is made, we should embody our professed beliefs.

What's your preferred process? What kind of evidence feels most important for you?

It's beyond the scope of this book or my own experience to present the scientific argument of a Francis Collins, the philosophical treatise of a C. S. Lewis, or the theological case of a Timothy Keller. Besides, as foundational as reading like that can be, I've found that the majority of seekers find their way to God in wildly different ways—each suited, no doubt, to our individual needs and nature. For you, it might take years of careful, scholarly investigation. For someone else, it might take one prayer, one encounter with an angelic presence, one dream, one scripture, one moment when heaven seemed to open up and speak your name.

Just be sure you are genuinely focused on testing your hypothesis, not—in the guise of a diligent search—actually committed to nonaction and self-protection. We can easily behave like we're in a court of law. Rather than accepting convincing evidence, we hold out for undeniable proof. There's a difference. One is a creative, proactive posture; the other is a defensive posture. This is especially true when we consider owning a life-changing truth for ourselves.

Jesus illustrated this point with his story of a hungry, sore-covered beggar named Lazarus who died and went to heaven, and a rich man who died and went to Hades. In Jesus's story, the suffering rich man looks up "far away" and sees Lazarus in comfort by Abraham's side. The rich man calls out to Abraham for relief, but Abraham gently reminds him it's too late for that.

So the rich man tries another approach:

> "[The rich man] answered, 'Then I beg you, father, send Lazarus (who was revived from being dead) to my family, for I have five brothers. Let him warn them, so that they will not also come to this place of torment.'
>
> "Abraham replied, 'They have Moses and the Prophets; let them listen to them.'
>
> " 'No, father Abraham,' he said, 'but if someone from the dead goes to them, they will repent.'
>
> "He said to him, 'If they do not listen to Moses and the Prophets, they will not be convinced even if someone rises from the dead'." (Luke 16:27–31)

In effect, Jesus is asking his audience, "How much evidence do you need?" The rich man wants Abraham to send his family proof from the other side of God's purposes, but Abraham reminds him that there was already sufficient evidence on Earth.

Do you understand the rich man's request? I do. In fact, somewhat like the rich man, I have often wondered why all people are not given a dramatic spiritual experience like mine to convince them of God's existence. But how much proof would it take to persuade a person who doesn't want to be persuaded? In a nod to what would happen later at his own resurrection, Jesus said, in effect, "Yep, well that kind of evidence doesn't exist." It is not surprising to me that so many people have profound spiritual experiences and turn to God only when something dramatic happens in their life that exposes the illusory nature of control. Perhaps they develop an illness that does not respond to treatment, a traumatic injury forces them into the intensive care unit, or a loved one dies unexpectedly.

While these are all common reasons and excuses for not forming a hypothesis or pursuing a spiritual life, believing in God is not usually an intellectual problem. Some people just don't want to believe. They don't want to yield to God or change their behavior. Being a casual person of faith feels good and is easy. Rather than feeling accountable to living the way God would have us live, we choose our actions and effortlessly forget the times we yelled at someone, gossiped about a friend, flirted with a coworker, or blurred the ethics of a business deal. Trusting God with our future also compels us to release our own expectations, and most of us would prefer to understand God's plan before agreeing to it.

Fortunately, as spiritual beings having a physical experience (see Chapter 3), you and I can count on the Spirit of wisdom and comfort to be with us in our search. I promise that you'll discover, as millions have before you, that if your heart is open to God's leading, and you are willing to sincerely look, you *will* find sufficient evidence to trigger a personal spiritual change. In fact, in Jeremiah 29:13 and Proverbs 8:17, God makes it clear that He *wants* to be found.

NOW, FORM A TESTABLE HYPOTHESIS

If forming a personal hypothesis to guide you sounds like high science to you, don't let the unfamiliar term throw you off. A hypothesis is simply an organizing tool to help you get your work done, the beam from a lighthouse to help you navigate across an ocean of data. To write a hypothesis and set about to confirm or deny it is, in its own way, an act of faith on the part of the scientist. He or she sends up a trial balloon to see what will happen. It's time to see what the facts bear out.

I recommend keeping things simple and direct. For a life that warrants living with absolute trust, your hypothesis could read something like "God is real and present" or "God's promises are true."

That's it. Now you know what you're testing. Now you're ready to collect data on your way to a really big prize—a radically new way of seeing and experiencing your life with God.

ACTIONS AND REFLECTION STEPS TO HELP YOU "LOOK BEYOND"

For each of these steps, write your responses in a journal or other record. That will invite you to be thorough and allow you to return to them again and again for contemplation and prayer.

1. Have you ever put your faith to the test in a thoughtful, openhearted way? If so, what was the result? What result would you most want from the evaluation process of looking beyond?

2. What emotional obstacles, rooted in your own story, have played the greatest part in keeping you from trusting God with all your heart, soul, strength, and mind?

3. What intellectual obstacles have exerted the strongest influence in keeping you from experiencing absolute trust?

4. What kind of evidence will you need to trust God completely with your life?

5. What is your working hypothesis that you want to test against the information you'll gather? Write it out.

Chapter 15

STEP 2: LOOK AROUND

Collecting Evidence from the
Natural World and Other People

"I can see how it might be possible for a man to look down
upon the earth and be an atheist,
but I cannot conceive how he could look up into the heavens
and say there is no God."

—ABRAHAM LINCOLN

What does it mean to collect evidence for a spiritual search? Does it mean sitting through endless sermons, reading weighty tomes, retiring to fast and pray for a month at a hermitage? It could. But that's not where I'd start.

In this chapter, we look around at both our physical world and life experience for signs that a supernatural, loving God is hiding in plain sight. After all, if God and the supernatural are everywhere present, couldn't we expect to see hints of that sparkling like diamonds in all directions?

What do you see when you look around? Not on a particularly special day, but on an ordinary one. Allow me to answer that question from my own life.

Living in rural Wyoming as I do, I'm reminded all the time that nature is full of divine evidence, pulsing with mysteries. Out my bedroom window, I see the silhouette of a solitary tree in the distant field. Often, an eagle or osprey perches solemnly in its branches, and I am always moved by its majesty. This is also the direction of my son's grave, and I almost always think of him when I look in this direction.

When I look out the kitchen window, I see aspen and cottonwood trees, ranchland, and mountains. I may see the chickens running around, and I often see (and hear) elk, moose, foxes, and coyotes. I occasionally see ermines. Depending on the season, horses or cattle are likely to be grazing in the field beyond our fence.

Looking toward the front of our house, I see our pond, which attracts herons, ducks, and geese. Mornings and evenings, I see trout rising to the surface to feed on the latest hatch of insects.

Inside our house, my glance often goes to the many photos of my family and of our adventures together. Every photo is a testament of grace, and I'm grateful.

I usually bicycle to work during the warmer months. Along the bike path, I see all sorts of nesting birds, but mostly robins, tanagers, and mountain bluebirds. I see their babies begin to fly. I notice when the flowers begin to blossom and smell their sweet fragrances. I luxuriate in the gift of breath and happily feel the warmth of the sun. No matter what the day brings, exercising always makes me feel great.

In the fall, I watch the aspens changing color. It always fascinates me to remember that a grove of aspen trees are genetically identical because they tend to be one enormous organism, linked together underground by a single, extended root system. That's why the leaves in an aspen grove all turn yellow within hours or days of one another. It always makes me think of how interconnected we all are.

These are some of the things I see routinely. On any given

day, I can choose to overlook them and let them fade into the background of my life, or I can choose to see God's handiwork within their details.

This chapter invites you to wake up to God in your day. Not the best, most miraculous, most "spiritual" day you ever had—just your ordinary day. What do you see in the world around you, in the human story unfolding through time, in your friends' experiences? Where do you notice God's fingerprints? Where might the proofs of heaven be peeking through in your life?

It's all so easy to miss!

LOOK AT NATURE

I believe if we study the world with intellectual honesty, it is reasonable to conclude there *must* be a God. The universe is breathtakingly complex. More astonishing still is that this complexity exists in a state of perfect balance, never spinning out of control into chaos, which I take as evidence in plain sight of a careful and intricate design.

If you find an old watch in an attic keeping perfect time, would you assume that random chance assembled it and gave it purpose? Likewise, we know the stones in an ancient wall didn't arrange themselves with such precision. A painter's vision and design are obvious on every canvas, and we follow footprints in the forest knowing they will lead to the deer. The psalmist knew this when he wrote, "The heavens declare the glory of God; the skies proclaim the work of his hands. Day after day they pour forth speech; night after night they reveal knowledge" (Psalm 19:1–2).

Seeing God around you might be as straightforward as doing the math.

Analytics came easily to Douglas Ell, a man with math

and physics degrees from MIT, a master's degree in theoretical math from the University of Maryland, and a law degree from the University of Connecticut. He was a self-proclaimed atheist who treated God as a joke, feeling intellectual disdain for the very concept. But when he mathematically evaluated the (im)probabilities of events in the natural world, his long-standing atheism gave way to bold faith in a Creator God. He wrote:

> *At one point, the math nerd in me could not help but calculate, literally on the back of an envelope on an airplane, the fantastic improbability that a single functional protein was ever created by accident in the entire history of the universe. I was thunder-struck—it was an "Aha" moment. I remember staring at the calculations in disbelief—couldn't others do the math, and see what seemed obvious? It was a "no-brainer." At that moment, I knew modern science supported belief in God.*[1]

Practice mindfulness as you pass through creation today—whether you find yourself on a crowded sidewalk, in a noisy hallway at school, or driving to work. Look around—at the rain, the wind in the trees, an icicle, the waves on the beach, a ladybug on a rose.

LOOK AT THE HUMAN BODY

Your body, whether young or old, consists of something like forty trillion cells, or about five hundred cells for every bright star in the Milky Way. Your body has been described as the most advanced structure in the known universe.[2] So, for a refresher in our proximity to miracles every day, the wonders of your own physical being make a compelling place to start.

Sometimes when I'm in a routine surgery I find myself

thinking about the astonishing complexity and perfection of the human body. In my practice as a spinal surgeon, I might be doing a spinal injection one day, disc replacement surgery the next, and fusing bones together on a different day. But whether it is working in the operating room or treating patients in my office, I am keenly aware of the fact that *I* don't actually heal anyone; neither does any physician, for that matter. What I do is to invite healing, preparing the way for injured bones and tendons to do the work of healing on their own. I never fail to be amazed at a body's ability to heal itself and to always try to get back to a more functional state.

The more I learned in medical school about the intricacies of the human body, the more clearly I saw the pattern and presence of a divine order. And I am not alone in this understanding. Despite the widely held belief that scientists are hostile to religion or that science and religion are incompatible, a recent study showed that nearly 36 percent of scientists have no doubt about God's existence.[3]

Like many accomplished scientists, Dr. Francis S. Collins found no reason to postulate the existence of any truths outside of mathematics, physics, and chemistry, and he was comfortable in his atheism—until he went to medical school and focused on genetics. The more he learned, the more his beliefs changed. Now the former director of the Human Genome Project and current director of the National Institutes of Health (NIH), Dr. Collins believes, "DNA is God's language, and the complexity of our bodies and the rest of nature is a reflection of God's plan. The God of the Bible is also the God of the genome. God can be found in the cathedral or in the laboratory. By investigating God's majestic and awesome creation, science can actually be a means of worship."[4]

What do you see in the innocence and beauty of a newborn? What do you see in the miracle of your own two hands? There are so many ways to wake up to the supernatural all around us.

CONSIDER FOUND TREASURES

You probably have a bible somewhere in your house—maybe several. But when you open it, do you remember that even as a historical document, it is one of the world's great wonders?

We "look around" at our physical experience in a historical sense when we try to corroborate biblical places, people, and events by reading ancient writings and studying the records of archaeological discoveries. Relics discovered during digs often provide physical historical evidence of specific biblical details. A 1906 expedition, for example, discovered evidence supporting the existence of the Hittites, a people previously unknown outside the pages of the Old Testament—and therefore assumed to be apocryphal. These archaeologists discovered the ruins of Hattusas, the ancient Hittite capital at what is today called Boğazköy, as well as a vast collection of Hittite historical records that are consistent with biblical records.

There is historical evidence of a great flood during the time Noah would have lived. Mesopotamians, Egyptians, and Greeks all recorded stories of a great flood in Hebrew times. Even the list of Sumerian kings from 2100 BC is divided into those who ruled before a great flood and those who ruled afterward. In 2012, master's students in the Department of Physics and Astronomy at the University of Leicester demonstrated mathematically that the instructions given to Noah in the book of Genesis would actually result in a boat that could not only float but also could support the weight of even more animal species than those that inhabited the earth at the time of Noah.[5]

Findings have also validated geographic details of biblical sites such as Jericho, Haran, Hazor, Dan, Megiddo, Shechem, Samaria, Shiloh, Gezer, Gibeah, Beth Shemesh, Beth Shean, Beersheba, and Lachish. The geographic specificity used in the Old Testament would suggest that the Bible was not meant to be merely metaphorical or allegorical.[6, 7]

LOOK AT ONE EXTRAORDINARY LIFE

We have abundant evidence that the supernatural stepped into the human story in physical form when Jesus came to Earth. Whatever your understanding of the divinity of the rabbi from Nazareth, the astonishing power of his teachings to change lives and redirect the course of nations has never been equaled.

The story of Jesus is not just Christian fiction. The ancient writings of Roman historian Tacitus confirmed the historical existence of Jesus when he reported on Emperor Nero's decision to blame the Christians for the fire that had destroyed Rome in AD 64. He wrote:

Nero fastened the guilt . . . on a class hated for their abominations, called Christians by the populace. Christus, from whom the name had its origin, suffered the extreme penalty during the reign of Tiberius at the hands of . . . Pontius Pilatus, and a most mischievous superstition, thus checked for the moment, again broke out not only in Judaea, the first source of the evil, but even in Rome . . .[8]

This record is thought to validate the physical existence of both Jesus Christ and Pontius Pilate. Further, scholars speculate that the phrase "a most mischievous superstition" refers to the Christians' belief that Jesus rose from the dead.

Pliny the Younger was the Roman governor of Bithynia in Asia Minor during the first century after the death of Jesus. In one of his letters to Emperor Trajan, dated around AD 112, he asks Trajan's advice about the appropriate way to conduct legal proceedings against those accused of being Christians. At one point in his letter, Pliny relates some of the information he has learned about these people:

> *They were in the habit of meeting on a certain fixed day be-*
> *fore it was light, when they sang in alternate verses a hymn to*
> *Christ, as to a god, and bound themselves by a solemn oath,*
> *not to any wicked deeds, but never to commit any fraud, theft,*
> *or adultery, never to falsify their word, nor deny a trust when*
> *they should be called upon to deliver it up; after which it was*
> *their custom to separate, and then reassemble to partake of*
> *food—but food of an ordinary and innocent kind.*[9]

Josephus, a first-century Jewish historian, also mentions Jesus when he describes the condemnation of one "James" by the Jewish Sanhedrin. This man, says Josephus, was "the brother of Jesus the so-called Christ."[10]

COLLECT THE WISDOM OF OTHERS

But what about present-day evidence of God among us? You read this book, at least in part, to get more information about that. For the same reason, I encourage you to collect heaven- and miracle-related stories from others in our own day.

As a way to understand the significance of this sort of evidence, consider what you would think about the cheeseburgers at your local café if two or three friends said it served the best-tasting cheeseburgers in the country—their words probably wouldn't make much of an impact. If fifty people told you the same thing, you might consider trying one. If one hundred people echoed this conviction, you would definitely try one for yourself. If one or two million people raved about your local café's cheeseburgers, you wouldn't even need to try one—you would be convinced this claim must be true.

A 2009 study conducted at the Pew Research Center demonstrated that more than 30 percent of Americans say they have "felt to be in touch with someone who has already died," and nearly half of all Americans claim to have had a religious or mystical experience (defined as "a moment of sudden religious insight or awakening"), including 18 percent of self-described atheists, agnostics, and the secularly unaffiliated. What's more, 13 percent claim to have seen or sensed the presence of an angel in the previous year, and at least 5 percent have had a near-death experience.[11]

This data would lead to an estimate of more than 100 *million* people who have had a deeply spiritual experience, including 15 million with a history of an NDE. Using the analogy of your local café, one shouldn't even need a personal experience to accept the truth of that spiritual reality.

Ask your friends about the "coincidences," or "synchronicities," that have occurred in their lives. Ask them about answered prayers, and spiritual experiences of any kind that they still value. Ask if they've ever experienced a miracle or seen an angel. You may be surprised to learn how many of your trusted friends have had deep spiritual experiences that they keep to themselves, like both Justin and Cindy did in the following two stories:

I worked for the phone company when I was a young man and got electrocuted one day when I was up on a telephone pole. The first thing I remember was looking down from somewhere in the sky and seeing one of my buddies doing CPR. I felt so peaceful and surrounded by God's love. When I started moving down a bright path, I recognized my grandpa. He told me to "go back," and suddenly I was in the ambulance. I tried to tell my wife about this, but she told me that it was just because I hit my head. I never told anyone else until now, and that was thirty-two years ago.

—Justin, Fort Worth, TX

When I was three years old, I fell off a dock when no one was looking. I didn't know how to swim and immediately sank to the bottom of the lake. I had the most loving encounter with Jesus. He held my hand while we talked but then told me I couldn't stay.

Suddenly, I popped to the surface right by the shore. My brother laughed and said I was lying when I told him I fell in and met Jesus. So I kept it to myself for many, many years. I remember this like it was yesterday and have never forgotten how much love I felt.

—Cindy, Midland, MI

Read other published accounts of NDEs, miracles, visitations, and encounters with angels. (I am not suggesting that you read these accounts with blind acceptance; some authors will purposely exaggerate the truth—or outright lie—for their own purposes, but you can begin by measuring them against the "quality checklist" I mentioned in Chapter 10.) Taken independently, most stories can be picked apart at their edges. And if you put two of them side by side, they will differ. But if you read ten of them, you will find striking commonalities. The more accounts of spiritual presence or intervention you hear or read, especially from sources you trust, the more you can trust the evidence you collect. As the volume of evidence increases, so does your ability to trust your conclusions.

As you "look around" at the world and the many stories of others, I am confident that not only will you find ample evidence that God is real and His promises are true, but your awareness of God's work in the world will fundamentally change. Rather than just seeing musical notes written on a piece of paper, you will begin to hear the music of heaven on Earth.

ACTIONS AND REFLECTION STEPS TO HELP YOU "LOOK AROUND"

For each of these steps, write your responses in a journal or other record that invites you to be thorough and allows you to return to them again and again for contemplation and prayer.

1. Look out of every window of your house, dorm room, or apartment. Keep looking until you see evidence of the supernatural. What is it?
2. What helps you most to "wake up" to God and the supernatural in your day? Is this a onetime event, or do you make it a practice?
3. If you could capture the truth about God that you see most clearly in a photograph of the Milky Way, what would it be?
4. When you look at the human body, what evidence of a trustworthy God do you see?
5. When you look at the historical record, including the Bible, what evidence of a trustworthy God do you see?

What evidence do you see that argues against a trustworthy God?

6. What evidence have you gathered from others about
   heaven- and miracle-related stories in their lives (including coincidences, synchronicities, visitations, dreams,
   angels, and NDEs)?

Chapter 16

STEP 3: LOOK WITHIN

Finding Signs of God's Presence in Your Own Story

"The best and most beautiful things in the world cannot be seen or even touched; they must be felt with the heart."

—HELEN KELLER

I've noticed that certain times and places seem to heighten my receptivity to the reality of heaven. Have you? I'd point to travel, solitude, immersion in nature, time at a spiritual retreat center. These can shake us free of our routines in a way that we become more sensitive to the divine. I've found the same to be true of both times of sorrow and times of celebration.

The date June 21, 2014, stands out in my memory because something happened that day to remind me that I'm never alone and that God's grace is always present and available.

That year my husband and I were traveling in the Turks and Caicos Islands. By the time we returned to our tiny hotel room at the end of the day, we were exhausted—not just from the physical activity of the day, but also from the pain and emotional strain of deeply feeling our loss. You see, it was the five-year anniversary of our oldest son's death. Looking for distraction while we showered and dressed for dinner, we turned on the little television. As the set powered up, we were shocked at what we heard coming over the airwaves: my voice!

An interview I had done with Randi Kaye on *Anderson Cooper 360°* was airing at that very moment. That alone was an amazing synchronicity. On the broadcast, I happened to be in the middle of explaining the joy God taught us to feel, even in the midst of our pain. What could have been an increasingly challenging day for us turned into an opportunity for even more joy as we embraced this small miracle and felt the warm embrace of God's love.

I believe we all are created to feel heaven breaking through. But sifting through the static of daily living to find the "signal" in the noise takes effort. Socrates famously declared that the unexamined life is not worth living. I'd reframe his adage here to say: "The *examined* life is priceless, because our experiences are containers holding the treasure of revealed wisdom—if we look." The verb *examine* is active, implying focused resolve and intention. We need to make time to meditate, listen, and watch.

This chapter invites you to be intentional about uncovering evidence of God's involvement and handiwork in your life story. I will first ask you to record the time line of your life, and I will offer ways to look for signs of God in your story. I will then close this exercise with a helpful list of prompts for where and how you can "look within."

FIRST, WRITE THE STORY OF YOUR LIFE

Create a simple chronology of your life that highlights significant events. This is not about producing a work of literature, by the way; it's about creating a helpful, private record. If you feel pressed for time, aim for a bulleted time line of key events—just one page, maybe two. Even if you fill an entire journal, what matters is that when you're done, you can sit back and see your story from start to now.

The main point is to prompt your memory to write down the major (and even minor) events that tell the story of your life. Your aim is still to gather information that might help you become more aware of how a loving, active, and present God has touched your life in ways that you might not have noticed at the time. But first you have to collect the facts.

Possibilities are practically endless, but your record could include: early memories; formative friendships; moves; schools attended; memorable disappointments; shining achievements; your first broken heart; marriages, divorces, and deaths in the family; your first job; and so on. You'll have to focus, and it may not be easy to get it all down, but you'll find it's well worth the trouble because the end result will constitute a map that shows you where to concentrate your attention.

Once your chronology is done, pick an event or time period in your life that has particular significance to you, and dig deeper. What made this time or event so important? What choices, circumstances, or coincidences made it what it was? What emotions did you experience most then? What people were pivotal in your life then? What obstacles did you face and overcome? Which ones still remain? Be specific. What caught your attention? Did you cross paths with someone who provided unexpected help or encouragement when you needed it the most? Did you experience any divine appointments, nudges, or small miracles? Were there times you stepped out in faith and flourished or were surprised to see the path made straight?

There is power in recording—in writing—the ways God has shown up in your life and proven His promises to be true. Transferring recollections from your brain to paper excavates forgotten events and crystallizes them in your consciousness.

THEN, LOOK FOR SIGNS OF GOD IN YOUR STORY

After you collect the facts you can begin to "look within" your life for meanings, connections, traces of that larger world of the spirit breaking into your story.

I've found that God shows up in small (or large) miracles, in hard-to-explain synchronicities, or in improbable encounters with people who nudged me toward my higher purpose. For me, God's sustaining grace is often most apparent during my darkest days when I have felt most abandoned and alone. Another reassurance from scripture pictures God like an eagle who "hovers over its young," spreading his wings to catch us and carry us aloft (Deuteronomy 32:11). Of course, we may be too distracted by our own distress at the time, but that is why it's so important to look back now.

Spend some time with your story once you have it sketched out. Go back through each event you've marked down. To look for signs of God there, go beyond the basic facts to reflect on how you felt and what you learned in the event or each encounter. Ask others who lived those times with you to help you recall some of the ways God clearly was—or might have been—present in your life.

Look closely at what psychologists and spiritual directors call liminal or threshold times, where you found yourself between one season of life and another, one identity and another. Times of significant loss, change, or brokenheartedness, for example, often leave us feeling the tension of liminality—hanging, as Franciscan Richard Rohr says, "betwixt and between" in our spirits. People of God down through the ages have felt that the spiritual world comes very close during those times—as the psalmist noted, "The Lord is close to the brokenhearted . . ." (Psalm 34:18).

Take time to meditate and pray as you process this step, asking God to open your eyes to see the kingdom of heaven hovering over your life.

Can you see patterns?

Can you think of why you may have missed them at the time?

Can you see outcomes now that only became apparent later?

I've found that the more I unearth evidence of God's fingerprints in my past, the easier it becomes to see those things as they happen in the present. That strengthens my commitment to lean on God for real transformation in my life.

We'll come back to the task of writing out and examining your life story, but first, let me give you three examples of where and how the presence of God often shows up.

THREE EXAMPLES

Seeing God in your disappointment or failure. Most of us have experienced an event that seemed like a great disappointment—even a disaster—at the time but proved to be a blessing later on. From our limited perspective, we often see only what didn't go as we planned and only gain clarity with the benefit of time. We look back months, years, or even decades later and say, "I couldn't see it at the time, but that was one of the best things that ever happened to me."

What appears to be a waste of time and effort can sometimes bear fruit years later. At other times, failure shows us we are traveling toward a dead end, and we are forced to redirect our course.

You might remember the story of Charles Colson, who plummeted from the heights of power to the depths of disgrace in the 1970s. Or so it seemed. Going to prison often feels like the ultimate failure, but the experience can also ignite transformation. It did for Colson. Once the special counsel to President Nixon, he was sent to prison for obstruction of justice on Watergate-related charges. As time passed, he found himself "increasingly drawn to the idea that God had put me in prison for a purpose and that I should do something for those I would leave behind." After his release, he founded Prison Fellowship, a Christian ministry that has become the world's largest outreach to prisoners, ex-prisoners, and their families.[1]

Seeing God in synchronicities. Did you know that there is not even a word for *coincidence* in Hebrew? The only equivalent is the word *mikreh,* meaning "a happening from God." Once you develop trust in God's promise of presence, you will believe as I do, that there is no such thing as a "meaningful coincidence," but there are many happenings from God.

As you look back, did you see or feel anything when a loved one died? Did an unexpected visitor leave you feeling mysteriously renewed and refreshed? Can you identify a time when you stepped out in faith only to be surprised at how your path was made straight and you flourished in the process?

Just as you asked your friends about their struggles, their experiences with miracles and angels, coincidences and synchronicities in the previous chapter, do the same of yourself now. We all experience synchronous events—"happenings from God"—that seem to be meaningfully related.

One day I could not stop thinking about my friend Cindy, whom I hadn't spoken with for a while. Rather than ignore this persistent thought, I picked up the phone and dialed. How could I have known that she had just been admitted to the hospital and was thinking of me at that very moment? For her, the synchronicity of my phone call became a source of comfort and encouragement. For me it was yet another reminder of the unshakable presence of God's grace. If we're faithful with small things, heaven breaks through for ourselves and others. We are doorkeepers.

Seeing God in closed doors. Life abounds with stories of times when the destinations we set for ourselves aren't where we wind up at all—thank God! So many things we wish for and work toward never come to fruition, and at the time we are severely disappointed. The door has slammed in our face. But in time we see that a different—and much better—door opened up. And as the new door opened up, so did wonderful opportunities to grow and flourish. As written in Proverbs 19:21, "Many are the plans in a person's heart, but it is the Lord's purpose that prevails."

He had been an award-winning jazz singer, but Willie Jolley was stunned and devastated one evening when, out of the blue, the owner of the nightclub where he performed regularly replaced him with a karaoke machine. With only $200 in his pocket, Jolley took a job with a drug-prevention program for at-risk youths. One of his new responsibilities was to give uplifting and motivational speeches to these kids, something for which he felt unprepared. As he observed the impact of his speaking, however, he discovered a previously hidden talent. In the twenty years since, Jolley has become a highly successful motivational speaker and author, perhaps best known for his declaration, "a setback is a setup for a comeback."[2, 3]

EVIDENCE OF THE UNSEEN

This chapter asked you to create a written chronology of your life, then begin to look for evidence of heaven there.

The following action and reflection questions will help you dig deeper into your story.

Consider making your review an ongoing process. For example, when you've done the work of excavation—unearthing clues in your past to God's ever-present hand in your life—set your journal aside for a few months. Let what you've learned percolate through your understanding. Then, when you're ready, pick up pen and paper again and dig some more.

As you become an expert witness to the testimony of your own life, you will see clear evidence that God showed up in surprising ways and confirmed that his promises are true.

ACTIONS AND REFLECTION STEPS TO HELP YOU "LOOK WITHIN"

1. How did God's presence and promises show up for you in the times described below? Include your answers in the written life story you began with this chapter.

   - Times of disappointment or failure
   - Times when you noticed synchronicities
   - Times when a closed door opened others
   - Times of celebrating a life passage—e.g., christening, baptism, graduation, wedding, birth, memorial service
   - Times of sorrow, pain, or loss
   - Times of utter joy
   - Times when you were confronted by great need or suffering in another person

2. Finally, how would you summarize what looking closely at your life story has shown you?

Chapter 17

—

STEP 4: FORM A CONCLUSION
Reevaluating Your Hypothesis and Making a Choice

"We must make the choices that enable us to fulfill the deepest capacities of our real selves."

—THOMAS MERTON

Winston Churchill once said, "Men occasionally stumble over the truth, but most of them pick themselves up and hurry off as if nothing had happened." Hurrying off, so to speak, from our quest to become more heaven-conscious here on Earth would be such a waste. Even if what you uncovered doesn't fit any preconceived notion or belief, even if you don't know quite what to do with important evidence from your past, don't rush off. You are standing on the threshold of a new way of living with God.

Step 4 in our quest to make heaven real in our life every day invites you to look at everything you have learned and apply it to your life. You have completed your personal investigation. Now it's time to gather your findings, form a conclusion, and—with a clear picture of what you now know to be true—choose to act.

With your search now complete, arriving at a conclusion and making a choice should be straightforward, even simple. Yet it requires that you bring your whole self to the page.

I understand that moving from collecting evidence to making a choice can be daunting. At this point, your posture toward your search shifts. You began by being mostly objective even while you were looking deeply into your own life, but now your approach becomes entirely subjective. You are no longer a case study; you're you, alive in the moment.

How will you allow what you've learned to change how you live now?

I can tell you from my own life that letting what we've learned from our spiritual experiences to change how we live takes more than collecting data. It takes courage. It requires commitment. You have to trust the sacredness of your own story as God gives you grace, and take the plunge. Put both feet in the boat.

GATHER YOUR FINDINGS

The truth is, now you have a lot to work with. Your journey began when you decided to follow my story—from that first powerful awareness underwater that I was safe in the embrace of Jesus to my return to my everyday life, and then through a careful exploration of what heaven teaches us about dying, miracles, angels, and God's loving plan for each of us.

You've also looked deeply into your own life. You have inspected the emotional and intellectual baggage that might be keeping you from opening your heart to absolute trust. You have looked around—at nature, history, corroborating stories from friends—and looked within to find the fingerprints of heaven on your life from the day you were born.

I firmly believe that any person who completes the faith-exploration exercise I've been describing will find convincing evidence of God's presence in the world and in his or her own life. The faith born of this process provides a logical way to make sense of what we observe in the world.

What are your findings telling you—not just in your thoughts and conclusions, but in your whole and deepest being? I hope you've found yourself coming alive to the Spirit, to God's insistent and loving presence throughout your life, and to the reality of God's kingdom in the now. I hope you are looking at the world differently—beginning to see, as the poet Elizabeth Barrett Browning wrote, that

> *"Earth's crammed with heaven,*
> *And every common bush afire with God . . ."*

REVISIT YOUR HYPOTHESIS

To guide your search, I proposed at the outset that you create a simple, testable statement about God's nature or his promises that you hoped would turn out to be true. This working hypothesis set the direction, the boundaries, and the end point of your search. Scientists use this approach all the time, of course, and for questions large and small. But I can't think of a search where one would need the help of a hypothesis more than in ours, where we're trying to find new insights in subject areas as vast and potentially elusive as God, heaven, and absolute trust!

I proposed something as simple as "God is real and present" or "God's promises are true." What hypothesis did you put to work for you, and how well has it held up during your search?

We can't really move toward applying what we've learned until we make the conscious decision to accept, reject, or revise our original hypothesis. That is precisely what Josh McDowell did when he set out to write a book that would refute

Christianity. In his classic book *Evidence That Demands a Verdict,* he writes, "After more than 700 hours of studying this subject, and thoroughly investigating its foundation, I have come to the conclusion that the resurrection of Jesus Christ is either one of the most wicked, vicious, heartless hoaxes ever foisted upon the minds of men, or it is the most fantastic fact of history."[1]

How might you revise or expand your original working premise, and why?

What is your new hypothesis?

FORM A CONCLUSION

Do you remember the encounter I had with Jesus in that beautiful field? I tried so hard to convey just how immediate, tangible, and convincing that conversation was for me.

I sat on the ground at one end of a long field. The field was filled with wild grasses gently swaying in a soft breeze. The entire area was bathed in the beautiful, golden glow of a late-afternoon sun. My arms rested comfortably on top of my knees. The ground beneath felt firm. The world around me glimmered with . . . what? Exhilaration! Yes, that's what seemed to fill creation.

In that setting, I encountered the person of Jesus for the second time (my first encounter was underwater, as my life slipped away). I wrote that he was "utterly, inarguably known to me."

I had no doubt it was Jesus and didn't need to ask his name. Asking would be like seeing my husband in the grocery store and, before starting a conversation, asking, "Are you Bill?"

Certainty like that changes a person. You just know what you know! Do you understand what I'm saying? Over and over, it's this kind of deep, almost physical conviction on which we hope to build our lives.

You probably know by now where your search has taken you, and whether or not you're ready to reach a conclusion. On the spectrum of conviction, between "confirmed skeptic" on the one hand to a "true believer" on the other, where do you stand?

We all approach this kind of a serious inquiry differently. That's why I asked earlier how much evidence, and what kind, you thought you would need to choose to trust God. I would describe the evidential path of this book as a combination of personal story (mostly mine), reports from other trustworthy sources, reliable texts, and medical and scientific data.

What evidence carries the most weight for you?

Materialists explain everything by physical causes, while rationalists believe that opinions should be based on reason and knowledge, rather than on religious belief or emotional response. A scientific rationalist—which I used to be—thinks scientific study and certainty in knowledge are the ultimate authority. They believe that with enough time, effort, and resources, everything can be explained by rational thought, rather than experience. And if it doesn't reduce to a scientific certainty, then it's probably not true and shouldn't be trusted.

While I fully support a rigorous exploration of spiritual matters applying the scientific method, I have personally seen its limits. Some truths will always exist outside the realm of science and intellectual understanding. We might identify the specific portion of our brain that shows increased activity when we feel love or compassion, but we will never prove *why* we should love or what it feels like to *be* loved. Likewise, we might identify the neurotransmitters that evoke the experience of spirituality, but we're not likely to learn from those neurons why they exist.

I have seen good people insist that somehow life or God

must answer *every* question before they open their hearts. This may appear to be intellectual integrity at work, but in my experience, it is more often a tactical convenience for a person who fears change, and in the meantime is holding God hostage to a test He may never choose to take. All researchers proceed from the known into the unknown based on what they know or think they might know at the time. Turns out, every intellectual quest requires steps of faith.

Based on the evidence you have gathered, and the hypothesis you have tested and refined, what could you now reasonably conclude about God in the key areas we've been exploring? For example, in considering the hypotheses we proposed at the end of Chapter 14,

1. Can you conclude that God is real and present in your life and in the world?
2. Can you conclude that God's promises are true?

If you've sincerely invested in this discovery process, you owe it to yourself to reflect patiently and deeply on your conclusions. Truly, almost everything of enduring consequence is at stake. As the beloved author A. W. Tozer famously declared, "What comes into our minds when we think about God is the most important thing about us."[2]

MAKE A COMMITMENT

I firmly believe that any person who completes the faith-exploration exercise I've been describing will find convincing evidence of God's presence in the world and in his or her own life. The faith born of this process provides a logical way to make sense of what we observe in the world and empowers us to make a life-changing choice.

Regardless of the details, *everyone* chooses a set of beliefs, whether we acknowledge doing so or not. Who will we choose to believe, and whose voice will we choose to listen to? We can accept the misrepresentations of the dominant culture, or we can believe our personal experience with God.

The next and final step is yours to take. How you commit to living now with absolute trust that God loves you and His promises are true is up to you. You might write out your decision and keep it posted prominently in your life. You might want to share your decision with close friends and ask for their support in prayer. You might begin with a simple prayer of dedication like the example that follows.

Look back on your life from the perspective of heaven and make your choice. You'll never regret it!

My Prayer of Dedication

Almighty, loving, and eternal God,
Thank you for opening my eyes to heaven,
and to the truth that you are always good.
You open my eyes to your miracles, large and small.
You show me that I can trust you absolutely.
You comfort me that death is not to be feared, and that
even in heartbreak and loss, beauty will blossom.
Now, keep me wide awake to the reality of heaven all
*   around.*
Renew my inner being so that I may live with joy,
serve others, and show your glory on Earth.
Lead me and guide me on the path you have prepared.
May your will be done today and always.
Amen.

Chapter 18

—

THE SWEETEST FRUIT ON EARTH

"Today is your day to dance lightly with life.
Sing wild songs of adventure.
Invite rainbows and butterflies out to play.
Soar your spirit and unfurl your joy."

—Jonathan Lockwood Huie

Whew! What a journey we have taken—from the depths of the river, to the glory of heaven, and back to the reality of daily life on Earth! Along the way, you have encountered the reasons I believe heaven and the supernatural are literally crowding in on our lives every day, even right now. We are not simply physical beings for whom "spiritual stuff" is a mere hope, a nice story, or a pleasing religious emotion. We are made for heaven, starting now. From birth, we are created to respond to the Spirit, to be touched by angels, to deeply long to live eternally with our loving God in the company of those we love.

My hope is that you have uncovered clear evidence from your own story to support this heaven-sized understanding. And based on your findings, I sincerely hope you have chosen to live with unshakable trust. If you find yourself even at the beginning of the trust transformation, I guarantee you are already experiencing a remarkable shift in your internal well-being—you have been surprised by joy.

Joy is not something you can chase, and unlike happiness, joy is not found within the world. David expresses the link between trust and joy. Take, for example, this joy-filled declaration in Psalm 92:4–5: "For you make me glad by your deeds, Lord; I sing for joy at what your hands have done. How great are your works, Lord, how profound your thoughts!" Even Solomon discovered that the happiness found in the world's pleasures is ultimately hollow, while the joy found in trusting God is rich and abundant (Ecclesiastes 2).

Joy is not just about one's own happiness, but comes from something bigger. It is not fleeting or based on one's momentary circumstances. It comes from your inner self rather than from something outside of you.

Joy is a state of being that blossoms from this trust in God's promises. It allows us to transcend our circumstances and find beauty, even in suffering and struggle.

Choosing to live with absolute trust is, indeed, the doorway to living a joy-filled life. But, in my experience, even joy takes tending. Its foundation can begin to weaken if we stop keeping the reality of heaven and God's amazing promises at the forefront of our minds. In this closing chapter, I want to share encouragements from my own life that can help you tend what is beginning to flourish in your life.

KEEP LOOKING UP

Mine is a family of Nordic skiers. Depending on where you live, that pastime might sound exotic, but Bill and I have raised our family beneath the towering peaks of the Grand Tetons. Nordic skiers tend to ski over hills instead of riding a lift or skiing around them, which makes the sport grueling and demands perfect technique. Sticky wax on the bottom of "classic" skis helps the skier propel himself or herself forward when he or she properly weights the ski and kicks backward. The more difficult and steep the conditions, the more important it is to center your weight over the waxed part of the ski.

Toward the end of a long race, exhausted skiers often begin to crumble and look down, but that spells trouble. Their shoulders sag, their weight shifts, and the ski loses traction. The resulting struggle and frustration can be eased by one simple action—looking up. This action automatically repositions a skier's weight and gives them the "kick" they need to propel themselves up and over the hill.

You can see where I'm going with this. When we face challenges, don't we tend to look down, feeling crushed by the weight of our concerns, sadness, and anxiety? I do. But without looking up, we miss the beauty. We don't notice the miracles, or sense God's nudge in critical moments. We wonder where God is and may not feel His presence as He walks next to us or begins to carry us.

We may forget that when God is for us, no one can be against us (Romans 8:31), and that He uses ordinary people to accomplish great things. We may lose the confidence to step out in faith and ignore those who say we are not good enough, talented enough, or smart enough to reach our dreams. We may forget that God does not call qualified people, but qualifies the ones He calls.

Without looking up, we forget that we are beloved children of God. We easily focus on our flaws instead of celebrating our unique combination of attributes and gifts. In questioning God's miracles, we feel discouraged instead of celebrating our intellectual curiosity and desire for experiential learning.

We forget that God's love is for all people—even the ones

we don't like or those who have hurt us. We forget that everyone carries a heavy burden and needs compassion rather than judgment, and we forget that we are meant to be agents of God's peace, love, and joy.

We will surely have seasons of happiness as well as heartache and without looking up we may overlook the opportunity to recognize that each experience is helping to shape us into the fullness of who we are intended to be. Even in the midst of chronic illness we need not lose heart, for as written in 2 Corinthians 4:16, we may be outwardly wasting away but inwardly renewed day by day. We can be assured that "our light and momentary troubles are achieving for us an eternal glory that far outweighs them all" (2 Corinthians 4:17). As we form an unshakable trust in His promises, the path before us becomes smooth, and we can rise above our circumstances.

When we stop looking up, we miss seeing the heaven that is within each day.

PRACTICING TO REMEMBER

To keep the reality of heaven and God's amazing promises at the forefront of our minds, I recommend creating memory markers throughout your day. I think of them as the stones the people of Israel used to build a reminder of God's faithfulness (Joshua 4) which, in the time of the prophet Samuel, became known as Ebenezers (1 Samuel 7:12). The Ebenezers we incorporate into our daily lives help us remember our journey of trust.

Of course, everyone has different routines and will respond to different types of Ebenezers, but I will share some of the ones that have worked for me.

Prayer always seems to bring my focus back to the trustworthiness of God and His promises. For me, prayer is primarily an act of praise, submission, and gratitude, knowing that God provides what we need, even if it is not necessarily what we want. In the midst of struggle, gratitude can feel in short supply. But even during such times, we can be grateful for the ways in which the struggle is molding us and producing an opportunity to grow into the person God would like us to be. While we might only see the next few steps ahead, God sees the entire path of our life. Making a gratitude list each day, even a short one, provides a reminder of God's love and helps us to remember to keep looking up.

Prayer also helps with discernment, and perhaps just as importantly, it helps to live with uncertainty. As we pray about our worries, joys, confusion, or decisions, God comforts us, and the Holy Spirit can direct our feelings, thoughts, and actions.

What prayer Ebenezer works best for you? You might like to pray while you're exercising or commuting. Or like me, you might start your day with prayer—before opening my eyes each morning, I silently recite the Lord's Prayer, and say "yes" to God.

> *Our Father, who art in heaven, hallowed be thy name,*
> *thy kingdom come, thy will be done,*
> *on earth as it is in heaven.*
> *Give us this day, our daily bread,*
> *forgive us our sins as we forgive those who sin against us,*
> *and lead us not into temptation, but deliver us from evil,*
> *for yours is the kingdom and the power*
> *and the glory, forever.*

I know that when I say yes to God, I say yes to the power of the Holy Spirit to show me God's will and provide wisdom, knowledge, faith, healing, and discernment.

SMALL BUT POWERFUL

I'm not sure how big those stone reminders were that Samuel and Joshua raised in ancient times, but I've found that "small" works for me just fine. Here's my list:

I have a *daily devotional* next to my bed that I read as I am brushing my teeth in the morning, giving my thoughts direction as I finish my morning routine.

As I walk outside, I take in a *full breath of mountain air* and feel gratitude for my ability to do so.

On my *morning commute,* I usually see the sun beginning to rise over the mountains on the other side of the valley. I never fail to be awed and I never fail to be grateful for where I live. I use that drive time to think about God's presence in my life and thank Him for His presence, grace, and love. I always ask that God helps me that day to see where He is leading me and how I can be of service to His kingdom.

Sometimes I will listen to *contemporary Christian music.*

I look for *synchronicities*—happenings from God. I try to be aware of angels and miracles. I strive to always have an open heart and spirit in every situation, considering if an event or encounter may have more significance than it seems on the surface.

I try to be aware of the *inner prompts*—those nagging thoughts and feelings that won't go away, even if I don't understand them. If I feel prompted to call someone, go somewhere, or say something, I make an effort to follow through. I often have no idea why I am being prompted, but I try to respond anyway.

I wear a cross on *a necklace beneath my shirt*. Whenever I feel it on my skin, I'm reminded of who I am, whose I am, and in whom I trust. I am reminded to keep looking up.

A *decorative cross* hangs in my office to remind me how I want to treat other people. Next to it, a wall hanging shows the words of Psalm 19:14: "May these words of my mouth and this meditation of my heart be pleasing in your sight, Lord, my Rock and my Redeemer."

I place *wall hangings and sticky notes* of my favorite sayings, quotes, and verses that remind me of God's promises in places where I am sure to see them: at my bedside, next to my bathroom sink, on the microwave oven, and on the wall behind my computer at work. In the Jewish tradition, this is the function of a mezuzah case, which contains a message from the Torah and is attached to doorways as a reminder of God's covenant.

Make your Ebenezers personal, even if they seem silly— why not? Each time I find *a coin on the ground,* I pick it up and read its imprint of "In God We Trust." I use these times to ask myself, *In this very moment, is my trust entirely in God's promises?* When I can answer affirmatively, I put the coin in my pocket and proceed with my day.

Think of your journal as your *memory book,* your personal collection of Ebenezer stones. And in the future, if you find yourself questioning God's nearness, you can always look back in your own memory book for reminders of his loving presence.

And finally, *join a faith community* that provides a regular reminder of the realities of heaven, as well as education and growth. Get involved in sharing yourself with others. Be a window through which God's light can illuminate the path for others. You may feel that your efforts are but a drop in the ocean of need, but the ocean would be less without your drop.

THE SWEETEST FRUIT—A JOY-FILLED LIFE

Unfailing. Unshakable. Trust offers a taste of heaven each day as our eyes and hearts are open to God's abundant love, grace, and miraculous presence in our world. As we keep God's promises foremost in our thoughts and choose to trust, life begins to change. With change, we begin to experience the fruits of this transformation—greater love, peace, patience, kindness, goodness, faithfulness, humility, and self-control.

Each of these is valuable and worthy but, for me, the very sweetest fruit produced from living with absolute trust is that of living with joy—joy in success and joy in failure; joy in unbridled happiness as well as joy in the midst of crushing sorrow. Where there is joy, there is God's presence. The joy of heaven is God's enduring gift to each of us, whatever our circumstances. Living a joy-filled life is the natural outcome of choosing to live in the truth of God's promises and offers a taste of what our loving God has in mind for our future . . . *right now.*

May the sweetest fruit of heaven be yours today, and every day of your life.

Acknowledgments

The writing of a book always involves the support and encouragement of many, and I am grateful to all who are, or have been, a part of my life. I would like to specifically thank:

Bill Neal, for your unwavering love, humor, and steadfastness. I could not walk this road without you.

Willie, Eliot, Betsy, and Peter Neal, without whom life would be very dull.

David Kopp, for believing I had something to say and helping me say it beautifully.

Elizabeth Gerdts, for always being a source of sunshine and laughter.

Keith Wall, for your way with words.

Betty Thum, for always showing how to love unconditionally.

Ann Bayer, Julie Connors, Susan Farquhar, Kelly Kiburis, Becky Patrias, and Linda Purdy, for more than fifty years of unconditional friendship.

Merle Long, for reminding me that big ideas do not need to be complicated.

Tom, Debbi, Jean, Kenneth, Anne, Rachel, Kayla, Isabel, Chad, Krista, Kyler, Bryson, Jenna, Tren, Linzie, Merle, Olivia, and Isaac Long for your love and for being such beautiful examples of what it means to live in one's faith.

Mel Berger, for perpetually offering cheerful encouragement.

Marta Lozano, Robin Steinmann, Heidi Anderson, and Alisha Keyworth, for keeping the wheels on the bus.

David Pfeifer, for being steadfast in your humor and friendship.

Father Ubald Rugirangoga, Rev. Dr. Paul Hayden, Rev. Mike Atkins, and Katsey Long, for your friendship, nurturing, and for being such great examples of joyful living.

Gil Malinkrodt, for your stories.

Joe, from California, and everyone like him, whose self-made barriers must crack before God's light can enter in.

READING GROUP GUIDE

You'd be hard-pressed to find a more fascinating, yet more far-reaching conversation than the one Dr. Mary Neal presents in this book! Take just some of her topics: What happens when we die? What is heaven like? Is there an angel near me right now? Do miracles happen? And what difference should our answers on such topics make in our life today? Happily, the scope and significance of such questions is more than matched by their promise. As Mary says, the truths that heaven reveals are intended to change how we live on Earth, and for the better. She writes, "My goal in this book is to help others live every day with *absolute trust* that God is good and his promises are true. Living in absolute trust is not just for people who've visited heaven. It's meant for everyone, changing what we feel, think, and believe."

We have created the Reading Group Guide to help you get the most from 7 *Lessons from Heaven*. When you gather with others who bring similar interests to a reading experience, you greatly enhance your ability to process and apply what you've read. Use the guide as a starting point rather than as a final exam. The best discussion groups don't insist on agreement, but invite and respect a range of thoughts and reactions to the materials. Listen carefully, share honestly, and open your heart to new insights. And most of all, enjoy!

—THE EDITORS

Introduction, This Changes Everything

1. Dr. Neal writes that as a surgeon, she had been conditioned by many years of medical training to be skeptical of anything beyond the scientific realm. "If it couldn't be measured, probed, x-rayed, and reproduced, then I couldn't rationally accept it." How would you describe the attitude or predisposition you bring to reading 7 Lessons from Heaven?

2. She also admits that putting personal spiritual experiences into words is difficult. Based on your own life, do you agree or disagree? Do you think a person's spiritual experience might actually be diminished when it is neatly wrapped up in approved religious language? Why or why not?

3. Have you or someone close to you had a near-death experience? If you're willing to talk about it—or at least try—please share it; others will be grateful.

4. If you had to identify one personal need or question that you *most* want this book to help you with, what would it be? Write it down or talk about it.

Chapter 1, River of Death, River of Life

1. This chapter begins with a fast-paced retelling of the accident that led to Mary's drowning and the experiences that followed. Were you able to relate to Mary's description of actually feeling quite peaceful in the moment of crisis? She says, for example, "I experienced no air hunger, no panic, and no fear." Share your reaction to Mary's account or a similar experience from your own life.

2. Have you ever felt the physical sensation of being held and comforted by Jesus or God? If so, describe.

3. As Mary describes what she saw in heaven, what thoughts, feelings, or questions occurred to you?

4. In heaven, Mary received heartbreaking news about the future death of her oldest son. Have you ever had a foresight or premonition that later proved accurate? If so, what was that like for you? How did it affect your understandings or your actions?

Chapter 2, Seeing My Life from Outside Time

1. The Bible says that, with God, one day is like a thousand years, and a thousand years is like one day (2 Peter 3:8). Do you ever feel that God's clock and yours run on wildly different rates? If so, discuss.

2. When you lose track of time, what are you likely to be doing?

3. Most people, even longtime believers, feel some anxiety about how Jesus will evaluate their lives. If this is true for you, would you say it's mostly a function of how you understand scripture, or mostly a function of being your own worst critic?

4. Mary writes that when her childhood prayers for her parents' marital reconciliation went unanswered, she felt betrayed and abandoned by God, and thereafter "discarded my childhood notions of a loving heavenly Father." Comment on that based on your experience? Do you sometimes think of prayer as presenting your wish list?

5. Talk about your perspective on what Mary calls the First Lesson That Heaven Reveals: *When we look at circumstances through the lens of heaven, understanding prevails, and the grace we receive from God is the same grace we can freely offer others.* Can you see how understanding another person's

history changes your perspective of them? Is this easy to do? Does your understanding of grace coincide with Mary's? Can you think of a time when your perspective of someone changed once you understood their personal history?

Chapter 3, We Are Both Physical and Spiritual Beings

1. Mary writes, "What I discovered when I stopped being a 'physical being' was that my capacity for experiencing everything around me—including and especially the profound love of God for me—radically expanded. Actually, I have never felt more alive than when I left my body far behind." What thoughts or feelings did you have as you read that?

2. "We are not human beings having a spiritual experience," wrote philosopher and priest Pierre Teilhard de Chardin. "We are spiritual beings having a human experience." Mary's version of the same insight is that we are mostly spirit encased in an "earth suit." Do you agree with this perspective? How might this insight affect your decisions and emotions today?

3. Mary writes that at the time of their passing from life on this earth, people "often see the beauty of heaven, a mother or mother figure, siblings, or people who weren't yet known to have died. They often talk about getting ready for a trip, ask about their luggage or tickets, describe angels, or mention the name of the person who is coming to get them." Does your family have a story of a deathbed visitation surrounding the passing of a loved one? Tell your story.

4. What is your personal reaction to what Mary calls the Second Lesson That Heaven Reveals: *Death is not to be*

feared, because death is not the end. It is a threshold where we leave our physical selves behind and walk whole into eternity.

Chapter 4, Sitting Next to Jesus

1. With no communications and no hospitals anywhere nearby, two men "just happened" to appear on the river-bank to help Mary's rescue party find a way out. More unexplainable coincidences followed. Have you had en-counters that seemed divinely orchestrated? Write them down, or talk about them.

2. Do you believe Mary when she says of the person sitting next to her on the rock that he was "utterly, inarguably known to me—he was Jesus." Why or why not?

3. Mary admits that she hesitated to tell others that her companion in the beautiful field was Jesus. "I wanted to deserve Jesus," she writes. What is your reaction to that desire?

4. Perhaps the best-known story Jesus told is of the return of the prodigal son (see Luke 15:11–32). Which brother in the story do you most identify with—the brother who "deserved" the father's love, or the son who didn't? Does Mary's experience with Jesus change anything for you?

5. Mary's Third Lesson That Heaven Reveals states: *Choos-ing forgiveness releases our burdens and frees us to live fully and joyfully in God's extravagant love.* Do you believe God's love has the ability to break the chains of your past disap-pointments and hurts? Do you see how this can set you free to enjoy the full and abundant life that God intends for you?

Chapter 5, Life Goes Further Than Science

For some readers, the science-focused content of this chapter may be off-putting, even unnecessary. For others, it will be the single most important chapter in the book. Here, Mary describes in some detail her quest to understand in physiological terms what happened to her. She organizes her research by question; for example, "Was it just my imagination?" and "Was it a seizure?"

1. Have you experienced something that left you baffled to explain rationally to yourself and others? What was it? How did you set about to find answers?

2. Mary writes, "I knew I needed to be methodical in my search for answers. After all the trauma I had sustained, could I trust my cognitive ability to help me reach reliable conclusions?" What safeguards can a person take who has reason to doubt his or her own reliability as the person asking the questions?

3. Do you find the scientific case that Mary builds convincing? Why or why not?

4. If you are a Christian or a follower of another faith tradition, have others suggested that your spiritual experiences and convictions might simply be creations of your own overactive imagination? If so, how have you responded?

5. Do you believe that science can—or eventually will—explain spiritual realities that people of faith call miracles? Or are you of the opinion that science can only go so far?

Chapter 6, Crossing Over and Coming Back

1. This chapter brings corroboration from scripture, history, and current accounts for the reality of near-death

experiences. All of the ten commonly shared phenomena cited here occurred in Mary's experience. Nevertheless, Mary sees your "reading this book as an act of courage." Do you agree or disagree? Explain.

2. In your own words, define an NDE as you understand it.

3. At least two biblical accounts seem to describe NDEs: the story of Elijah and the widow's son in the Old Testament (1 Kings 17:17–21), and Paul's journey to "the third heaven" (2 Corinthians 12:2-4). How well do these two experiences fit your answer to question #2?

4. Mary writes, "Skeptics often use these differences between individual details to question the validity of the NDE phenomenon." How do you respond to the variances in the experiences of others? Do you see it as a positive or a negative?

5. Have you ever experienced something that was so unusual or profound that it seemed to set you apart from others, in part because you felt unable to talk about it easily?

Chapter 7, A Guided Tour of Heaven

1. Were any of your assumptions about heaven changed by what you read in this chapter?

2. Describe what you imagine heaven to be like? How much has that picture changed since you were a child? How do you talk about heaven to your children, if you have them?

3. How do you feel about sharing heaven with people you don't want to be there?

4. Read the Bible's description of "a new heaven and a new earth" (Revelation 21:1–5). What do you find most personally appealing in this account? Does heaven matter

more to you now, or less, than it did ten years ago? Explain.

5. Share your personal reaction to what Mary calls the Fourth Lesson That Heaven Reveals: *Heaven is a reality, where we are made whole—no pain, no sorrow, no suffering—understanding prevails, relationships are reconciled, and we will be with God and our loved ones forever.*

Chapter 8, Miracles Are Always in the Making

1. Where do you stand on the reality of miracles today? Choose one and explain:
   a. I believe they used to happen, but no longer do.
   b. I believe they could happen, but don't.
   c. I believe small miracles happen today, but not at the scale we see in scripture.
   d. I believe miracles of any scale are just as real and possible today as ever.

2. If a miracle has touched your life in an important and memorable way, would you be willing to talk about it? If you experience a "nudge" or whisper as being from God, what is your typical response? If you act on the prompt, what outcomes have you seen?

3. Mary writes about the blooming Bradford pear tree and alpine rose. Do you take certain small signs or reoccurrences in your life as a nudge from heaven that God is present and at work in your life? Talk about it.

4. Do you feel that some people overly ascribe happy outcomes in ordinary life to the miraculous? What might be a downside to this outlook?

5. Share your personal takeaway from what Mary describes as her Fifth Lesson That Heaven Reveals: *Big miracles hap-*

pen sometimes; personal miracles happen often. God invites us to notice His miraculous presence all around.

Chapter 9, Angels Walk Among Us

1. Have you or someone close to you been "touched by an angel"? If so, what happened?

2. Sentiment versus strength—I love the line from Psalm 103 (at the top of this chapter) where they are described as "mighty ones who do His bidding."

3. If angels come from God to do God's business, why do you think angel encounters in the Bible so often strike people with fear?

4. Why do you think angels are often reported nearby when a person is about to pass from this life to the next?

5. Have you ever come to believe then or later that a person helping you was actually an angel? How did it affect your emotions? How did it affect your spiritual understanding?

Chapter 10, God Has a Plan

1. Can you recall a time in your life when you needed more intensely than usual a sense that a loving God was in control? What about your situation was most troubling? How did things resolve?

2. Jesus taught that we need not fear being unknown or uncared for by God (Matthew 10:29–31). Why do you think it's so natural for us to feel separate from, even abandoned by our heavenly Father?

3. Mary says, "I constantly try to sense where the Holy Spirit is leading." Would you say you are a person who looks for guidance "constantly," for even small decisions, or one

who tends to only ask for help with big decisions? Explain. Do you see a risk for leaning one way or another?

4. Do you relate to what Mary means when she talks about spiritual prompts? Share your experience.

5. On page 147, Mary writes her quality checklist for making a decision. What would your checklist look like, and how is it working for you?

6. In what area of your life are you currently most in need of clarity, or struggling most to say yes to God? From the perspective of heaven, what kind of advice would you give yourself?

7. Talk about your personal reaction to what Mary calls her Sixth Lesson That Heaven Reveals: *God has a plan for each of us—full of hope, purpose, and beauty—and He wants us to discover it.*

Chapter 11, Beauty Blossoms from All Things

1. The central question of this chapter is universally challenging: "If God is all-good, all-knowing, and all-powerful, why does he allow evil in the world?" Would you say your response to the question has tended to drive you toward God or away? Why? Have you noticed any change in your response over time?

2. The question of God's goodness in the face of evil seems unanswerable at times. Does Mary's story of the corn maze suggest a possible solution?

3. Mary proposes three pictures for how we can think about God's plan: a river, a cowriter, a handwoven rug. Which picture resonates most with your experience now?

4. If you've ever been in the midst of a painful, unwanted experience, someone has probably tried to encourage you with a statement like, "You'll be okay—God works ev-

erything out for our good" or "You'll understand why some day." Why can responses like that be unhelpful, even hurtful at the time?

5. Can you identify an experience in your past that felt entirely awful, wrong, and even cruel at the time, but that you see differently now? Talk about it. How did that experience shape your outlook now?

6. Share your personal response to what Mary calls the Seventh Lesson That Heaven Reveals: *In our mistakes and failures, tragedies and losses, God never leaves us. His goodness and love surround us. In His time, beauty blossoms in all things.*

Chapter 12, There Is Hope in the Midst of Loss

1. Have you experienced a premonition about something that came true? Do you believe it was coincidental, or a message from heaven? Talk about it.

2. Thinking back to your own experiences of loss, what gestures, actions, or words would you say brought you the most comfort? Explain.

3. We all want to live without regret. Why is actually accomplishing that so difficult?

4. Of her loss of her son, Mary writes: "Many days I wanted to stay curled up in bed, wanting only to be relieved of the pain, of existence itself. But I survived. . . . Even on my saddest day, the joy I found in God's promises never left me." Do you believe pain and joy can exist so closely together? If so, has that been true for you? Talk about it.

5. If you've been through grief, how has it affected your other close relationships? What have you learned from the experience?

6. In your own words, what is the promise of heaven for us in our grief?

Chapter 13, How to Live with Absolute Trust

1. Mary writes that "we're invited to lean wholly and confidently—in *absolute trust*—on God's unfailing goodness."
   If you were to apply a scale of 1 to 5 to show how much
   or how little you trust God's goodness (1 being little to
   not at all, 5 being a lot or all the time), how would you
   rank yourself today?

2. "Hope is like oxygen," writes Mary. Can you recall a
   time in your life when you felt hopeless? If so, what did
   that feel like? How did that affect your energy level?
   Your ability to make decisions? Your feelings about the
   future?

3. Some people think of faith as primarily about ascribing to
   the correct set of beliefs, or behaving religiously. There's
   nothing wrong with those things, of course, but why
   might that leave a person—in Mary's terminology—only
   partly "in the boat"?

4. "Faith becomes trust when we personally see evidence of
   God's presence in our own life, and act on it." Have you
   acted in trust for this reason recently? If so, share your
   experience.

5. Mary uses a picture of a footbridge over a ravine to il-
   lustrate what trust in God, or the lack of it, looks like.
   Where would you place yourself in relation to the bridge
   today? Why?

Chapter 14, Step 1: Look Beyond

1. Why might it be important to bring more than simply
   our intellect to a search for evidence of God in our lives?

2. Mary proposes a list of reasons that our past could be
   blocking our ability to understand and respond to God.

She describes these reasons as baggage. Pick one or two of the obstacles (baggage) that were true in your past. Would you say these obstacles blocked your progress in your spiritual life (a) entirely, (b) partly, or (c) very little or not at all? Explain.

3. Can you identify obstacles that you're finding particularly limiting or distressing in your life now? What would it take for you to get past this "baggage" and go free?

4. As you "look beyond" your life for evidence of God's loving presence, what do you see? What kind of evidence feels most important for you?

5. What working hypothesis have you decided to take with you as you collect evidence of God's loving presence and purpose in your life? If you're willing, please share.

Chapter 15, Step 2: Look Around

See also the suggestions for Actions and Reflection for this chapter.

1. Mary describes what she sees when she looks out her windows at home and on her commute. Look out your windows at home or on the way to work. Take the time to write down what you see. Keep looking until you see evidence of the supernatural. What is it? Any surprises or insights?

2. On the spectrum of "very aware" to "not very aware," how would you describe your level of attentiveness to signs of God or the supernatural in your typical day? What helps you most to "wake up" to God and the supernatural in your day?

3. If you could capture the truth about God that you see most clearly in a photograph of the Milky Way, what would it be?

4. When you look at the human body, what evidence for or against a trustworthy God do you find?

5. When you look at the historical record, including the Bible, what evidence for or against a trustworthy God do you find?

Chapter 16, Step 3: Look Within

See also the suggestions for Actions and Reflection for this chapter.

1. How did God's presence and promises show up for you in the times described below? If you're willing, choose one or two examples you can share with the group.

   • Times of disappointment or failure
   • Times when you noticed synchronicities
   • Times when a closed door opened others
   • Times of celebrating a life passage—e.g., christening, baptism, graduation, wedding, birth, memorial service
   • Times of sorrow, pain, or loss
   • Times of utter joy
   • Times when you were confronted by great need or suffering in another person

2. As you look closely at your life story, share what you find that you consider: (a) evidence of God at work in your life; (b) evidence that the supernatural world (angels, nudges and prompts, miracles, so-called "visitations") is always near; and (c) evidence that God has a plan and a purpose for you.

3. Does your inventory of your own life experiences suggest that you are becoming more aware and more responsive to God's presence over time, or less?

Chapter 17, Step 4: Form a Conclusion

1. In this chapter, Mary leads the reader in a summing up. You have completed your personal investigation. Now it's time to gather your findings, form a conclusion, and—with a clear picture of what you now know to be true—apply it to your life. What could change for the better almost immediately for you if you take this action?

2. Reread the Churchill quote that opens the chapter. Why is it so easy—when we encounter important, potentially life-changing insights about how to live well—to "hurry off as if nothing had happened"?

3. In the Gather Your Findings section, Mary describes her book as a discovery process, starting with what she learned in her near-death experience and from other sources, and continuing with what we, too, can learn. To what degree has reading 7 *Lessons from Heaven* been a discovery process for you? Share your answer, and explain.

4. How well has your reading and thinking supported your working hypothesis? How might you revise or expand your original working premise, and why?

5. Based on your reading and the evidence you've gathered, where on the spectrum of conviction, between "confirmed skeptic" on the one hand to a "true believer" on the other, would you now place yourself? (Use a scale of 1 to 5, where 1 represents "confirmed skeptic" and 5 represents "true believer.") How do you feel about your answer?

6. Based on your reading and the evidence you have gathered, what could you now reasonably conclude about God in the key areas we've been exploring? For example:
   • Can you conclude that God is real and present in your life and in the world?
   • Can you conclude that God's promises are true?

Chapter 18, The Sweetest Fruit on Earth

1. Mary writes, "We are made for heaven, starting now. From birth, we are created to respond to the Spirit, to be touched by angels, to deeply long to live eternally with our loving God in the company of those we love." To what degree do you agree with the author? Has reading 7 Lessons from Heaven changed your thinking? If so, how?

2. An Ebenezer is a physical and sometimes public reminder of God's faithfulness. Do you have Ebenezers in your life? If so, what are they? How often do you use them?

3. Which of the practical memory minders that Mary lists sound most inviting or helpful to you?

4. Would you say that joy characterizes your life (a) a little, (b) quite often, or (c) a lot? How do you feel about your answer?

5. Mary closes her book by making two bold claims. First, she writes that "the joy-filled life is the natural outcome of choosing to live in the truth of God's promises." Then she adds that the joy-filled life "offers a taste of what our loving God has in mind for our future . . . *right now.*" How could the promise of these assertions help you as you make decisions and face challenges in the week ahead?

Notes

Chapter 3

1. Pierre Teilhard de Chardin, cited in *The Joy of Kindness* (1993), by Robert J. Furey, p. 138.
2. Carla Wills-Brandon, *One Last Hug Before I Go: The Mystery and Meaning of Deathbed Visions* (HCI, August 2000).
3. Mona Simpson, "A Sister's Eulogy for Steve Jobs," *New York Times,* October 30, 2011.
4. Peter and Elizabeth Fenwick, *The Art of Dying* (Bloomsbury Academic, 2008).
5. P. Fenwick, H. Lovelace, and S. Brayne, "Comfort for the Dying: Five Year Retrospective and One Year Prospective Studies of End of Life Experiences," *Archives of Gerontology and Geriatrics* 51, no. 2 (2010): 173–79.
6. S. Brayne, et.al., "Deathbed Phenomena and Their Effect on a Palliative Care Team: A Pilot Study," *American Journal of Hospice and Palliative Care* 23, no. 1 (2006): 17–24.
7. William Barrett, *Deathbed Visions* (Methuen & Co, 1926).
8. Cokeville Miracle Foundation, *Witness to Miracles, Remembering the Cokeville Elementary School Bombing* (Pronghorn Press, 2006).

Chapter 4

1. Lewis B. Smedes, *Forgive & Forget: Healing the Hurts We Don't Deserve* (HarperOne, reprint ed., April 12, 1996).

Chapter 5

1. Eisenberg, Mickey, ed., *Resuscitate!: How Your Community Can Improve Survival from Sudden Cardiac Arrest* (University of Washington Press, 2009).

2. Susan J. Diem, John D. Lantos, and James A. Tulsky, "Cardio-pulmonary Resuscitation on Television—Miracles and Misinformation," *New England Journal of Medicine* 334 (June 13, 1996): 1578–82.

3. Akihito Hagihara, et. al., "Prehospital Epinephrine Use and Survival Among Patients with Out-of-Hospital Cardiac Arrest," *JAMA* 307, no. 11 (2012): 1161–68.

4. Wendy Russell, "A Nonbeliever's Near-Death Experience," *Blogspot*, May 2013, http://www.wendythomasrussell.com/blog/a-nonbelievers-near-death-experience.

5. Ibid.

6. Jessie Davis, "Mystery of Death Solved: DMT Is the Key," *Wondergressive,* February 1, 2013, http://wondergressive.com/death-solved-by-vestigial-gland/.

7. J. P. Orlowski, "Prognostic Factors in Pediatric Cases of Drowning and Near-Drowning," *Journal of the American College of Emergency Physicians* 8, no. 5 (May 1979): 176–79.

8. Suominen, et. al., "Impact of Age, Submersion Time, and Water Temperature on Outcome in Near-Drowning," *Resuscitation* 52, no. 3 (2002): 247–54.

9. L. Quan, et. al., "Association of Water Temperature and Submersion Duration and Drowning Outcome," *Resuscitation* 85, no. 6 (2014): 790–4.

10. P. van Lommel, et. al., "Near-Death Experience in Survivors of Cardiac Arrest: A Prospective Study in the Netherlands," *Lancet* 358 (2001): 2039–45.

11. J. Allan Hobson, *The Dreaming Brain* (Basic Books, 1988).

12. P. M. H. Atwater, "Children and the Near-Death Phenomenon: Another Viewpoint," *Journal of Near-Death Studies* 15 (1996): 5–16.

13. M. Morse, *Closer to the Light: Learning from the Near-Death Experiences of Children: Amazing Revelations of What It Feels Like to Die* (Ivy Books, reprint ed., 1991).

14. Y. Miyashita, "Inferior Temporal Cortex: Where Visual Perception Meets Memory," *Annual Review Neuroscience* 16 (1993): 245–63.

15. I. Fried, "Auras and Experiential Responses Arising in the Temporal Lobe," *Journal of Neuropsychiatry and Clinical Neurosciences* 9 (1997): 420–28.

16. P. van Lommel, *Consciousness Beyond Life: The Science of the Near-Death Experience* (HarperOne Publishing, 2011).

17. N. J. Cohen and H. Eichenbaum, *Memory, Amnesia, and the Hippocampal System* (MIT Press, 1993).

18. L. R. Squire, "Memory and the Hippocampus: A Synthesis from Findings with Rats, Monkeys, and Humans," *Psychological Review* 99, no. 2 (1992): 195–231.

19. Cohen and Eichenbaum, *Memory, Amnesia, and the Hippocampal System*.

20. T. Y. Kao, et al., "Hypothalamic Dopamine Release and Local Cerebral Blood Flow During Onset of Heatstroke in Rats," *Stroke* 25 (1994): 2483–86.

21. Lee A. Phebus, et al., "Brain Anoxia Releases Striatal Dopamine in Rats," *Life Sciences* 38, no. 26 (1986): 2447–53.

22. S. A. Barker, et al., "LC/MS/MS Analysis of the Endogenous Dimethyltryptamine Hallucinogens, Their Precursors, and Major Metabolites in Rat Pineal Gland Microdialysate," *Biomedical Chromatography* 27, no. 12 (2013): 1690–700.

23. Rick Strassman, *SDMT: The Spirit Molecule: A Doctor's Revolutionary Research into the Biology of Near-Death and Mystical Experiences* (Park Street Press, January 2001).

24. "DMT, broken down and described," April 23, 2012, https://tmblr.co/Zq_O-wKB3IrL.

25. Pipp UK, "Amazing Airbulb Invention: An Experience with DMT (ID 62835)," May 24, 2007, erowid.org.

26. James L. Kent, "Psychedelic Information Theory: Shamanism in the Age of Reason" (PIT Press, Seattle, 2010).

27. Kevin Williams, *Nothing Better than Death* (Xlibris Corporation, 2002).

Chapter 6

1. G. Gallup and W. Proctor, *Adventures in Immortality: A Look Beyond the Threshold of Death* (McGraw Hill, New York, 1982) pp. 198-200.

2. *The Republic* (Dover Publications, April 2000).

3. *The Dialogues of Saint Gregory the Great,* translated in 1608 (Evolution Publishing & Manufacturing, 2010), book 4.

4. *The Republic* (Dover Publications, April 2000).

5. "St. Gregory the Great," introduction by Edmund Gardner, *The*

Dialogues of Saint Gregory the Great, translated in 1608 (Evolution Publishing & Manufacturing, 2010), book 4.

6. Personal communication and K. C. Sharp, *After the Light: What I Discovered on the Other Side of Life That Can Change Your World* (William Morrow & Company, 1995).

7. Personal communication.

8. Laurelynn Martin, *Searching for Home: A Personal Journey of Transformation and Healing After a Near-Death Experience* (Cosmic Concepts Pr, August 1, 1996).

9. Cohen and Eichenbaum, *Memory, Amnesia, and the Hippocampal System.*

10. Kenneth Ring and Sharon Cooper, *Mindsight* (iUniverse, 2nd edition, 2008).

11. Anita Moorjani, *Dying to Be Me* (Hay House, 2014).

12. Victor and Wendy Zammit, *A Lawyer Presents the Evidence for the Afterlife* (White Crow Books, 2013).

13. Todd Burpo, *Heaven Is for Real* (Thomas Nelson Publishing, 2010).

14. Comments made at an IANDS meeting, August 2014.

15. B. Greyson and I. Stevenson, "The Phenomenonology of Near-Death Experiences," *American Journal of Psychiatry* 137, no. 10 (October 1980): 1193–96.

Chapter 7

1. Cherie Sutherland, *Within the Light* (Bantam Books, 1995).

2. P. M. H. Atwater, *The Big Book of Near-Death Experiences* (Hampton Roads Publishing, 2008).

3. P. M. H. Atwater, *Beyond the Light* (Carol Publishing Group, 1994).

4. Ann Price, *The Other Side of Death* (Ballantine Books, 1996).

Chapter 8

1. Susan Spencer, "Just a Coincidence, or a Sign?," *CBS News,* October 12, 2014.

2. Christy Beam, *Miracles from Heaven* (Hachette Books, November 2015).

Chapter 9

1. Betty Malz, *Angels Watching Over Me* (Fleming H. Revell Co., 1986).

2.   Marilynn and William Webber, *A Rustle of Angels* (Zondervan Press, 1994).

3.   Joan Wester Anderson, *Where Angels Walk* (Ballantine Books, 1992), pp. 60–62.

4.   Elaine Jarvik, "Cokeville Recollects 'Miracle' of 1986," *Deseret News,* May 15, 2006.

5.   Sue Bohlin, *Angels, the Good, the Bad, and the Ugly—The Range of Angelic Activity* (Probe Ministries, 1995).

Chapter 10
1.   Brother Andrew, et. al., *God's Smuggler* (Spire, 1960).

Chapter 11
1.   P. M. H. Atwater, *Children of the New Millennium* (Three Rivers Press, 1999).

2.   Leslie Weatherhead, *The Will of God* (Abingdon Press, 1987).

3.   C. S. Lewis, *Mere Christianity* (HarperCollins, 2011).

Chapter 12
1.   Ibbotson, Eva, *The Dragonfly Pool* (Puffin Books, reprint ed., 2009).

Chapter 13
1.   http://www.integratedcatholiclife.org/2015/09/daily-catholic -quote-from-st-francis-de-sales-11/.

Chapter 15
1.   Douglas Ell, *Counting to God: A Personal Journey Through Science to Belief* (Attitude Media, 2014).

2.   El Bianconi, et. al, "An estimation of the number of cells in the human body," *Ann Hum Biol,* no. 6, (Nov–Dec 2013): 471.

3.   Ecklund, "Religious Understandings of Science," presentation at the annual American Association for the Advancement of Science, February 16, 2014.

4.   Francis Collins, *The Language of God: A Scientist Presents Evidence for Belief* (Free Press, 2007).

5.   "Hurrah! The animals could have floated two by two according to physicists," posted by the University of Leicester Press Office, April 3, 2014. "Noah's Ark would have floated . . . even with 70,000 animals," Sarah Knapton, science correspondent for *The Telegraph,* Friday, April 3, 2014.

6. *Christian Research Journal* 27, no. 2 (2004). Israel Finkelstein and Neil Asher Silberman, *The Bible Unearthed: Archaeology's New Vision of Ancient Israel and the Origin of Its Sacred Texts* (The Free Press, 2001).

7. Kathleen M. Kenyon, *Digging Up Jericho* (Ernest Benn, 1957), *Excavations at Jericho,* vol. 3 (British School of Archaeology in Jerusalem, 1981).

8. Tacitus, *Annals* 15.44, cited in Strobel, *The Case for Christ,* (Zondervan Publishing House, 1998).

9. Pliny, *Letters*, translated by William Melmoth, rev. by W. M. L. Hutchinson (Harvard Univ. Press, 1935), vol. II, X:96, cited in Habermas, *The Historical Jesus.*

10. Josephus, *Antiquities,* 200, cited in Bruce, *Christian Origins*, p. 36.

11. Pew Research Center, "Many Americans Mix Multiple Faiths," December 9, 2009.

Chapter 16

1. Charles W. Colson, *Born Again: What Really Happened to the White House Hatchet Man* (Conservative Press Incorporated, 1976).

2. Willie Jolley, *A Setback Is a Setup for a Comeback* (St. Martin's Griffin, 2000).

3. Liz Davis, "Willie Jolley: The Comeback King," Success.com, January 2, 2010.

Chapter 17

1. Josh McDowell, *Evidence That Demands a Verdict* (Here's Life Publishers, Inc., rev. ed., December 31, 1986).

2. A. W. Tozer, *The Knowledge of the Holy: The Attributes of God: Their Meaning in the Christian Life* (HarperOne, October 6, 2009).

About the Author

DR. MARY NEAL authored the acclaimed bestselling book *To Heaven and Back,* has been a featured guest on many national television and radio shows, and is a sought-after inspirational speaker. She is a board-certified orthopedic spinal surgeon, has published in academic journals and books, is a member of numerous medical professional organizations, and currently practices in Jackson Hole, Wyoming.

#1 *NEW YORK TIMES* BESTSELLER

TO *Heaven* AND BACK

*A Doctor's Extraordinary Account
of Her Death, Heaven, Angels, and Life Again*

A True Story

MARY C. NEAL, MD

A kayak accident during a South American adventure takes one woman to heaven—where she experienced God's peace, joy, and angels—and back to life again.